DOG
&
Puppy
CARE

DOG
&
Puppy
CARE

A COMPREHENSIVE GUIDE TO THE
CARE AND WELFARE OF YOUR PET

Maggie & Alan White

PHOTOGRAPHY BY PADDY CUTTS

Bramley Books

To Kerry and Schula

This edition published 1996 by Bramley Books

ISBN 1-85833-552-3

Conceived and produced by Linda Doeser Publishing Services
Editorial Director: Linda Doeser
Editorial Assistant: Ann Dean
Veterinary Consultant: John Oliver, BVETMED, MRCVS
Illustrations: Samantha Elmhurst

Design by Kingfisher Design, London
Art Director: Pedro Prá-Lopez
Designers: Frank Landamore, Frances Prá-Lopez

Printed and bound in Italy

Cover design: CLB International

CONTENTS

INTRODUCTION

We have tried with this book to help you pick your way through the possible minefield that choosing, buying and caring for a dog can become. You cannot think too hard or too long before choosing your dog. You would be amazed to learn how many puppies pass through dogs' homes or are re-homed by the many dog rescue societies because their original purchasers did not take enough time or seek enough advice to make an informed decision. A dog bought on the spur of the moment could turn out to be one of the worst decisions you ever make.

First, you must make sure that the type or breed of dog you choose will fit in with all the family's wishes and needs. Do you have enough space at home or will one extra body fill your house to bursting point? Do you want a large or small dog and do not forget that long-coated breeds need more grooming than those with short coats – and will shed more hair on the carpets. Any breed you choose will have to be all things to all people: Dad might want a dog to take on long walks at weekends or to take hunting. Mum, on the other hand, may want a breed that will not make too much work or get under her feet in the kitchen and the children are probably looking for dog they can play with. With over 120 recognized dog breeds, you can certainly be spoilt for choice. Conversely, you should not think that you will like every single breed. Just like people, the looks and personality of a particular breed might have tremendous appeal for one family, while another may find them distinctly off-putting.

Having considered all the general pros and cons, remember finally that you will probably be gaining a devoted friend and companion for at least the next 12 years, who will be totally dependent on you for food, friendship, guidance, grooming, exercise, fun and, most of all, love. If you can provide these in full measure, everything you expect from your dog will come back to you, many times over.

Choosing a puppy is an important decision. With proper care and some good fortune, it will probably be sharing your home and your life for 12 years or more.

I

THE NEW PUPPY

Having done all your homework (see pages 68–109), you have finally decided which breed is the right one for you and you now want to set about finding the perfect puppy. This does not, of course, mean that you should rush out and buy the first example of your chosen breed you encounter. Rather, you should see as many as possible before making a decision.

WHERE TO FIND YOUR PUPPY

There are a number of specialist magazines devoted solely to dogs, published both weekly and monthly. These contain useful information and lots of advertisements. You can also look at more general newspapers which sometimes also advertise puppies. Many dog breeders and owners disapprove of this method of finding homes for puppies, but as long as you exercise diligence and caution, it is possible to find a good quality and well-cared-for puppy through general newspaper advertisements.

You will undoubtedly find your local veterinarian a mine of information. If there is a breeder living nearby, the veterinarian will almost certainly know of him or her.

Do not be afraid to approach an owner who is out walking the breed that appeals to you. Most dog owners are more than willing to talk about their beloved pets and can provide lots of useful information, often including the names and addresses of the breeders from whom they bought their own pets.

Local and national dog shows are also often a good source of information. They will certainly give you the opportunity to see a number of examples of many different breeds. However, shows in the U.K. are simply for looking and talking, not buying, although you can sometimes buy from shows in the United States.

You may also know of someone whose bitch – either pedigree or non-pedigree – has been mated and who is looking for homes for the puppies once they are independent.

Avoid the Pet Shops

Unfortunately, some people still think that the best place to find a new puppy is a pet shop, but this is really not the case. Few responsible pet shops now sell animals, other than birds, fish and small rodents, as they recognize that a shop is not a suitable environment for baby creatures, such as puppies and kittens.

Puppies that do end up in shops are usually too young to have left their mothers and are prone to infection, as they will not be old enough for the necessary inoculations. Pedigree puppies in a shop are often the runts of a litter that a breeder has been unable to sell elsewhere. However, some pet shops carry notices for

Warning

Although all the people who work devotedly with rescue dogs try to ensure that they are properly socialized and no danger, many dogs will have some kind of behavioural problem, ranging from the very minor to the more serious. This is especially true of an animal that has suffered cruelty or neglect. Patience, kindness, understanding and a lot of love will usually overcome any problems the dog may have and you will eventually be rewarded with the most affectionate and devotedly loyal of companions.

RESCUE DOGS

Every year thousands of dogs arrive in breed rescue centres and general rescue kennels – most of them through no fault of their own. Some were bought in haste or because they were cute puppies and have later lost their appeal. Some come to rescue agencies as a result of marital break-up when partners have had to move to smaller homes or places where they cannot keep a dog. Some arrive when their owners die. All these situations are very distressing for the dog; it has lost its home and family and has no idea why.

Rescue services also take in dogs that have been starved, beaten or appallingly neglected by their owners and it continues to amaze – and delight – all those who work with them that these animals can trust,

love and give unlimited devotion to a new, caring owner.

Most breeds have a rescue co-ordinator and a list of these is produced by the Kennel Club. If you decide to take a pedigree rescue dog, the breed rescue co-ordinator will question you at length about why you want a rescue dog and may want to check you and your home for suitability to that particular breed and its requirements. Similarly, the rescue services who care for mongrel waifs and strays will want to ensure that you fully understand your chosen dog's needs and the responsibilities of caring for an abandoned animal. It is very important to everyone involved in dog rescue to make sure, when placing a dog, that it is going to the right home.

It has already undergone the stress and pain of losing one home and they do not want the same thing to happen a second time.

A dog from a rescue centre will have been given a general health check-up and any necessary treatment, including inoculations and worming. Neutering both bitches and dogs is widespread throughout the rescue services in the hope of preventing more unwanted puppies.

Most rescue agencies depend heavily on volunteer workers and have very limited funds. You do not usually have to pay for your dog or puppy, but a realistic contribution towards the work of the centre is always warmly welcomed.

puppies looking for good homes and some may even know of reputable breeders of pedigree puppies with whom they can put you in touch.

The following list may help you find the puppy you require:

- notice board in the local veterinary practice
- advertisements in local newspaper
- advertisements in local shop windows
- advertisements in the national press
- advertisements in specialist dog magazines
- Kennel Club information office
- re-homing agencies
- for a pedigree breed – go to a dog show and see all the varieties available.

THE RIGHT DOG

Dogs can live for a very long time – 12 years or longer in most cases – so it is essential that you make the right choice in the first place. Sadly, many people take on a dog or puppy as a 'spur of the moment' decision and, if things do not work out, the poor creature will end up in a rescue agency as another unwanted pet.

Your decision to share your life with a dog is a personal one and the whole family should be involved in the final choice. Never give a puppy as a birthday or Christmas present unless you are absolutely sure that it is wanted.

First you must decide what breed of dog would best suit you and your lifestyle and whether you want a pedigree or a non-pedigree. For instance, it is no good choosing one of the giant breeds, such as a Great Dane or a St Bernard, if you live in a small flat or apartment, or a dog that needs a lot of exercise, such as a Dalmatian, if you do not have the time. Take plenty of time to choose the correct dog and remember that the tiniest puppy will increase considerably in size as it grows up. If you attend local dog shows, you will see a vast selection of dogs. The owners are always very willing to talk to you and tell you everything there is to know about the breed,

This delightful little creature will probably grow up to be a charming adult dog of which any owner could be proud, but there is no knowing how big it will eventually be or what sort of personality and characteristics it will develop.

NON-PEDIGREE

FOR
• usually free or for a donation to charity
• available in a multitude of shapes, colours and coat lengths
• puppies from a rescue agency will probably have had at least their first inoculations and adult dogs will be fully inoculated
• adult dogs from a rescue agency will probably have been neutered
• may be shown, although only under limited circumstances

AGAINST
• no knowledge of parentage – other than, sometimes, the mother
• no knowledge of inherent behaviour patterns
• no knowledge of how the puppy will look or how big it will be when adult
• a puppy from a private home will need a full course of inoculations

including its requirements for exercise, grooming and other specific needs.

For people who cannot abide the thought of walking in the countryside, who live in the centre of town or are elderly, one of the Toy breeds may prove to be a good choice. Most of the smaller breeds can make devoted companions and certainly do not behave like 'toy dogs'. Most have hearts like a lion and are quite capable of standing up for themselves and their owners when called upon to do so. However, if you have a young, boisterous family, maybe one of the breeds that is a little more ruggedly constructed will fit the bill. Most breeds get on well with children, especially if, having been introduced as a puppy, they grow up with them.

Pedigree or Non-Pedigree

If you are thinking of having a dog simply as a pet, you may prefer a mongrel or cross-breed. (A cross-breed is the offspring of two pure-bred but different breeds, whereas a mongrel may have any number of different breeds in its ancestry.) If you also want to show your dog, there are shows that have a section for dogs of unknown parentage. Whatever you decide, the dog will be with you for many years, so it is sensible to weigh up the pros and cons for both types.

Pedigree puppies, like these Cavalier King Charles Spaniels, are a 'known' quantity. In this case, you would be safe in assuming that these puppies will grow up to be hardy, good-natured, loving towards children and friendly towards other household animals. You would also be right to assume that they are prone to ear canker, tend to develop slightly runny eyes and need regular grooming each day.

PEDIGREE

FOR
- available in all colours, shapes and sizes
- known family background
- predictable size, shape and personality of the adult dog
- may be shown and bred from (if no restrictions on registration document)
- price tag sometimes includes insurance

AGAINST
- can cost a lot of money
- some breeds are more demanding than others
- may need specialist grooming care, depending on the breed chosen

CHOOSING YOUR PUPPY

It is important to see the entire litter, together with the mother, when you visit the breeder to ensure that the puppies are learning to socialize and that all is well and healthy with the entire family.

It is sensible to visit the litter from which you are contemplating buying a puppy at least twice. You should always choose your puppy in person. Do not take children with you on your first visit; they will want the first puppy they see or all of them! Stand quietly and watch the litter play. Are all the puppies fairly even in size? Do not forget, an adult male dog is taller and heavier than a female dog. Do not pick the smallest one just because you feel sorry for it.

Do the puppies appear to be content? Is the puppy pen clean? Puppies do have accidents, but that is no excuse for not keeping them clean and tidy. Have they been wormed and had a preliminary set of vaccinations?

What you should be looking for, be it dog or bitch, is a bright bold puppy that is more than ready to investigate you. Do not forget to take note of how the puppy's mother reacts to you. This is a good indication of how the puppy's temperament will develop.

Beware of breeders who do not allow you to see the whole litter, together with the bitch. Also, avoid breeders who have several different litters available, with no sign of the mothers. These are usually unscrupulous 'puppy farmers', who take

As they begin to grow up, the puppies should be full of mischief and happy to play together, finding all kinds of fun as they learn more about the world they live in.

little care of the dogs' health and so any puppy you choose may not be in the best of health.

Most breeders are busy people, often with a job as well as a family and a home to run, so do give them them some consideration:

- Telephone first for an appointment.
- Make sure that you see the mother with her puppies.
- Do not be surprised if you are not allowed to handle the puppies; they are very vulnerable before they have been inoculated.
- Do not make appointments to see several breeders on one day. It is just possible that you could carry an infection from one household to another.

Finally, do not let anyone else make up your mind for you. Take your time. It is your decision and you will have to live with it – it is hoped, happily – for at least the next 12 years.

Dog or Bitch?

Most puppies are destined to become a much-loved family pet and so, unless you are contemplating purchasing a pedigree bitch for breeding purposes, there is little to choose between a male and a female.

Personality

Although there are always exceptions, as a general rule the personality of a pedigree breed is a known quantity and this is fully explained in Chapter 6 (see page 68). Non-pedigree puppies, often with an unknown father, are not so predictable and their personalities and characters will depend more on the environment in which they grow up.

Meet the family

Ideally, the whole canine family should be pleased to meet you. The puppies should be active, playful, outgoing and interested in all that is going on around them.

When choosing your puppy, select a friendly extrovert, rather than one that is timid or shy; the latter may just be of a more retiring disposition, but it could equally suggest behavioural or health problems – or both.

Waiting lists

It is worth finding out about and visiting local dog training classes and puppy 'playschools' before your puppy is old enough to need them or even before it arrives. These classes are often very popular and may have a waiting list, so the sooner you sign up, the better.

PLANNING AHEAD

Do not waste the time between choosing your puppy and the big day when you go to collect it. There are lots of important preparations to make. For instance, you must decide where the puppy will sleep and what it will sleep in. What will it eat, what dishes will you use and where will you put them? Have you found a veterinarian? The list could go on, but the following points are worth bearing in mind.

- The puppy should have its own bed and blanket in a warm, draught-free room. You do not have to buy an expensive bed or basket. Often a cardboard box lined with old newspapers and a blanket is the best choice until your puppy is past the chewing stage.
- Make sure that there are no electric cables within chewing range.
- Some sort of floor covering other than carpet is essential – puddles and carpet do not mix well! A good supply of old newspapers is invaluable.
- You will need a feeding bowl and a water bowl that cannot be tipped over.
- The breeder will advise you about which type of food the puppy is used to, so ensure that you

HEALTH CHECKS

Pedigree puppies will sometimes have had a full veterinary check-up before going to their new homes, but you can tell a great deal about their general condition by looking at them closely and assessing their level of well-being. Look at the eyes, teeth, ears, abdomen, coat and anal area. Also, take a note of the whole body and demeanour of the dog. The skin should be quite loose and move easily over the skeleton and there should be a moderate layer of fat beneath it. If you are allowed to pick up a puppy and it feels comfortable and slightly heavier than you expected, this is usually a promising sign.

Take a note of the surroundings. If they are unhygienic, the puppies are at risk of infection.

Bright eyes, an alert expression, a clean smooth coat and a soft, plump abdomen are all indications of a healthy, happy puppy that would be a pleasure for anyone to own.

have some available. The puppy's diet sheet should also give advice on quantities and frequency of meals, as well as details of any nutritional supplements that have been used.

- Other useful things to buy before your pup arrives include a small comb and soft brush. The sooner your puppy gets used to being groomed, the more it will enjoy it later on.

- Also consider a soft collar in order to acclimatize it to wearing something around its neck. An identity tag is essential once the puppy is old enough to go outside.

- Finally, what about a toy or two (see page 62)?

Wearing a soft collar will help your puppy get used to the unfamiliar sensation of something around its neck before it is old enough to go outdoors, when a collar – and identity tag – will be essential.

Look for the following points and you should find that you have a fit and healthy puppy:

- The eyes should be bright and clear, with no sign of inflammation or discharge.

- The teeth should be clean, the gums pink and the breath sweet smelling.

- The ears should be clean inside, have no unpleasant smell and no sign of a discharge.

- The stomach should be plump but soft: any firmness may indicate worms. A swelling on the abdomen may also indicate a hernia.

- The coat should be clean, shiny and free of parasites and scaly patches.

- The anal area should be clean and dry with no sign of discharge or diarrhoea.

- The general appearance should be that of a happy, healthy and well co-ordinated puppy.

Finding a Veterinarian

Neighbours are a good source of information about veterinarians. Business telephone directories also list all the local practices. Visit the practices that you are considering to establish opening times, vaccination charges and schedules and any other health concerns.

Most waiting rooms contain a good supply of leaflets giving useful information on caring for your dog, as well as details of the many canine insurance companies and the levels of benefit they offer. Many practices also sell nutritionally balanced puppy and adult dog food, flea sprays, worming tablets, collars and other equipment.

Register your puppy with the veterinarian immediately. Do not wait for an emergency, as formalities may delay treatment. Equally, if the veterinarian has already met your puppy and has seen how it normally behaves, it will be easier for him to diagnose a problem if the puppy is a little unwell and acting unnaturally.

Pet carriers

If you are collecting your puppy on foot or travelling by public transport, use a proper pet carrier. Inexpensive, fold-flat, cardboard carriers are available from most veterinarians and pet stores. Line the base with a sheet of plastic and a thick covering of old newspaper. This not only makes the puppy more comfortable, but also prevents the cardboard from disintegrating – with dire consequences – if the puppy urinates on the way home. It is also sensible to support the carrier from underneath as well as holding it by the handle.

It is never safe to carry a puppy, that may be frightened by unfamiliar noises and people, in your arms. It could squirm out of your grasp – with a tragic outcome.

BRINGING YOUR PUPPY HOME

The great day has finally arrived and you are off to collect your puppy. Have you prepared properly? Just think: this little bundle of fur has probably never been outside its own home before, not to mention gone on a car journey.

Try to ensure that your puppy's first day with you is a quiet one. Birthdays and Christmas are usually noisy and busy and this can be frightening for a young animal. It is best to collect the puppy in the morning in order to give it as long as possible to settle into its new home before you go to bed and leave it alone.

If you are collecting your puppy by car, ask another adult to come with you to keep the puppy and the driver safe during the journey home. Try to avoid taking the entire family. Have a couple of large, old towels to put over your knees and some paper towels in case the puppy is travel sick or urinates on the way home.

On arriving home, put the puppy into its new bed. It will probably stay there until it feels a little more confident. The family can help here: no loud noises, no rushing around and lots of gentle words of encouragement. Do not let children rush in and make a terrific fuss, which will probably frighten a puppy already having a somewhat traumatic change in its young life. And do not leave the puppy in a room on its own.

SAFETY

Once your puppy has settled in and feels a little more confident, it will want to explore its new home and will, undoubtedly, be up to mischief. Like all young animals, including the human variety, it is not aware of the many potential dangers.

Keep the following list in mind for the first few weeks:

- Look out for your feet – it is so easy to tread on a small animal.

- Close doors carefully: it is easy to slam a door and hurt or even kill a puppy. Keep outside doors and all windows shut.

- Unplug electrical appliances, where possible, and keep an eye on cables and flexes – puppies can chew through them.

- Move breakable items out of reach.

- Poisonous house plants should be removed or kept out of the puppy's reach.

- Keep sewing materials, wool and elastic bands in a safe place; all of these are dangerous to puppies if ingested.

- Keep your puppy indoors until it has received the full course of vaccinations.

- Make sure the puppy has plenty of company. It should not be left alone for long periods.

- Do not let the puppy near a staircase or, better still, block off the stairs with a gate.

After a couple of hours, try offering a little food, but do not worry if it is refused. Just take the food away and try it again later. Do not forget, this is all a very new and unnerving experience. It will not do any harm to introduce your puppy to the garden, taking it to the place you want it to use regularly. Lots of encouragement and you may just get the right result. Praise the puppy afterwards.

At first, there will probably be accidents, especially at night, so remember to cover the floor with newspaper just in case. The more you stick to a routine, ensuring the puppy is accompanied into the garden after every meal, the quicker it will become house-trained.

Puppies and the Family

An important part of your puppy's upbringing is the way it is introduced into the family. If you treat your puppy like a china doll, it will almost certainly grow up to be nervous, anti-social and frightened of its own shadow. On the other hand, a puppy that has been cuddled and played with is likely to grow up to be a well-balanced and loving companion.

To begin with, of course, you should not overwhelm the new arrival with too many people and too much noise all at once. Let it get to know the members of the family quietly and calmly, although this does not mean that children cannot play with it – if both parties want to. It is sensible to supervise children, at

A dog is the perfect friend, companion and playmate for children of almost every age.

Introducing a rescue dog

When choosing a rescue dog, you would be wise to ask about its past experience with children. Even so, extra vigilance when the new arrival meets the family is a wise precaution.

least to begin with. Young children especially can torment a puppy without even realizing what they are doing and should be taught not to tease it or pull its tail, coat or ears.

Visitors to the house should also be introduced to the puppy, as this forms part of the all-important socialization process. Puppies benefit from being handled from a very early age, as it helps them become accustomed to people. Conversely, rough or harsh handling can seriously hinder a puppy's socializing. So, too, can over-boisterous play sessions.

Above all, children should be discouraged from playing too strenuously with the puppy. Do not forget that this little creature is only a few weeks old and may never have even seen children before. Most importantly, respect the puppy's wishes; if it goes back to its bed and snuggles down to sleep, it is probably tired.

Owning two puppies is twice the fun and they also provide each other with companionship. This can be especially valuable when settling into their new home. At least something – or someone – is familiar.

Puppies and Other Pets

After it has been introduced to the family, the next big step for your puppy is to be introduced to and accepted by any other animal members of your household. How do you accomplish this? The quick and easy answer is do not worry about it. As long as it happens quietly, slowly and without your direct interference, all will be well. Nobody knows why, but animals seem to be able to integrate far more easily than humans. In any pack of animals, there is always a 'pecking' order and the position of any new arrival needs to be established to everyone's satisfaction.

A family cat will soon make sure the puppy knows its place. It is sensible to clip the cat's claws before you bring the new puppy home to avoid a badly scratched inquisitive nose. Introducing an adult dog, such as a rescue, may take a little more time and care. It is probably best to keep the dog on a leash to begin with and it is important to be sure that the cat has a means of escape or at least somewhere safely off the ground that it can jump onto.

Be firm that neither barking nor chasing is acceptable. Let the animals get to know each other but do not leave them together unsupervised until they have learned at least to tolerate each other. Usually they will become firm friends within a relatively short time.

A resident adult dog is more likely to feel slightly threatened by the new arrival than to be aggressive towards it. When introducing them for the first time, make a special fuss of the adult dog and

Dogs and cats often live together in perfect harmony, becoming playmates and good friends. It is usually the cat that becomes 'top dog' and the one that decides whether to accept the dog's invitation to play.

allow someone else to bring the puppy to it. Concentrate on the adult, ignoring the puppy yourself and they will probably get used to each other very quickly. The garden is a good place to effect this introduction. Before long, the older dog will be showing its new companion the 'ropes', but again, do not leave them unsupervised until you are sure that they will tolerate each other.

It is best to keep small pets, such as hamsters, mice, rats and gerbils, safely out of the way, especially if your puppy is one of the natural 'ratting' breeds, such as many of the Terriers.

Never neglect your current pets in favour of the new one; this can lead to jealousy and bad feelings among the pack. If anything, you should show more affection to your current pets than usual to reassure them that they have not been discarded in favour of the new arrival. At some stage there may even be the odd scrap, but do not panic: it will not be anything serious, just the cementing of newly-established relationships.

2

FEEDING

This will probably be your dog's favourite chapter! Eating is certainly something for which he needs no training and will do as often as possible if you let him (you should not). The dog's only requirement is that the food both smells and tastes good.

However, for you, the new owner, selecting the best way to feed your dog could cause severe headaches. There must be more than 100 different brands of dog food available. These, in turn, can be broken down into many categories: flavours, varieties, high-protein diets, low-protein diets, foods for obese dogs, dogs with illnesses, pregnant bitches, puppies – the list is almost endless.

Your dog will not care about the nutritional value of its food. As long it tastes all right, it will tuck in with enthusiasm whenever supper time comes round. Nevertheless, a properly-balanced diet is vital to a dog's health and general well-being.

If your dog is to stay healthy, it is vital that you feed it sensibly. If you fail to do so, you will soon end up at your local veterinarian with an ailing pet. Since people started to domesticate what was once a wild omnivore, the importance of feeding a sensible, correctly-balanced nutritious diet has become increasingly apparent. These days, with a multitude of different brands of dog food available, varying extensively in appearance, smell and composition, no one can honestly claim to be unable to find a food that suits his or her dog.

Correct Nutrition

When they lived in the wild, dogs were perfectly capable of feeding themselves properly, even if they did it unknowingly. Hunter-killers, they chased, caught and devoured their prey. Drinking from clean water sources and the additional consumption of wild fruits and grasses helped satisfy the requirements of a balanced diet. This once fearsome wild animal has long since been domesticated and the modern dog, even if it were capable, would not be permitted to behave in such a way. To stay healthy, the dog is now totally dependent on people to supply food to fulfil its dietary and nutritional requirements. An adult dog can survive on many different diets, but some are more suitable than others for maintaining good

AVERAGE DAILY FOOD REQUIREMENT

Dog: 40kg/88lb

Dried Food: 550g/18oz

Canned Food: 1100g/39oz (2 parts)

Mixer: 650g/23oz (1 part)

Dog: 20kg/44lb

Dried Food: 300g/10oz

Canned Food: 600g/21oz (2 parts)

Mixer: 400g/14oz (1 part)

Dog: 9kg/20lb

Dried Food: 180g/6oz

Canned Food: 400g/14oz (2 parts)

Mixer: 225g/8oz (1 part)

health. In fact, it is fair to say that a poor quality diet can considerably shorten a dog's life.

There are several constituents of dog food, all of which are important. Serious deficiency or excess of any of them can have a detrimental effect on your dog's health. These may vary from minor, tiresome complaints to serious, even life-threatening conditions, when intensive veterinary treatment may be required.

Carbohydrates

These are mostly contained in cereals, grains, potatoes, pasta, biscuits and bread. They supply most of the calorific content of the diet. In other words, they provide your dog with its energy, liveliness and vitality. They also constitute the 'bulk' of the food which is what stops your dog from feeling hungry again immediately after eating. They assist, too, in the normal passage of food through the digestive system.

Fats

These also supply calories and energy. They are essential for skin and coat condition; too little fat in the diet causes dry skin and a dull coat. Most importantly – for your dog – the amount of fat helps govern the texture of the food and imparts the flavour. It is essential that the fats are always fresh; apart from smelling disgusting, rancid fat can destroy the balance of a diet.

Vitamins

These are especially important for the growing puppy and dogs under stress, such as lactating bitches and working dogs. They perform many useful functions individually as well as reacting with the overall diet to provide essential nutrients. Among other vitamins, commercial dog foods usually contain vitamins A, D, E, B12, folic acid, pantothenic acid, niacin, thiamine, riboflavin and choline.

Supplements

If you are feeding your dog a well-balanced and varied diet, it is unlikely to need additional vitamins or minerals. Although you may *think* you are doing something helpful by providing vitamin or mineral supplements, you could actually damage its health through overdosing. Occasionally, it may be beneficial to provide additional nutrients – in the case of a pregnant bitch, a vegetarian or a very old dog, for example – but you should always consult your veterinarian first. Otherwise, you might end up doing more harm than good.

All proprietary brands of dog food contain the correct balance of nutrients or give advice on what, if anything, should be added to ensure that the food is nutritionally balanced. Labels and packaging often also include guidelines on the amount of food required by different-sized dogs. However, these are inevitably approximate and only you can judge the proper quantities for your particular dog.

Minerals

Minerals are important. Calcium is essential for bone growth and iron and copper are important for healthy blood. Most dog foods contain these, together with phosphorus and charcoal.

Proteins

Protein is as vital to a dog's diet as it is to a human's. The amount of protein in dog food governs the animal's daily life, its metabolism and capacity for work or exercise.

As food passes through the digestive system, the protein content is digested and broken down into amino acids, the building blocks of a healthy lifestyle. Dogs require over 20 amino acids, but the dog, being such a clever animal, can manufacture many of these itself or synthesize them from other components of its diet. In fact, only nine amino acids must be specifically included in the diet. A shortage of any of these will quickly result in deficiency symptoms.

TYPES OF FOOD

Always read the manufacturer's instructions on the packaging. Not all foods are 'complete diets'; some require supplements.

Fresh Food

Most dogs love fresh food, but it should also include a balanced mixer meal to ensure an adequate intake of vitamins and minerals. Many owners cook poultry or meat for their dogs once or twice a week and rely on the more convenient and scientifically formulated prepared dog foods for the rest of the time. Most dogs love raw meat, but it is best to keep to beef or lamb; poultry, pork and fish need cooking to destroy any harmful bacteria. Fish, poultry and chop bones are sharp or splinter easily and should always be removed before giving fresh meat to a dog. Liver, kidneys, heart and other similar meats should be given only once or twice a week.

VEGETARIAN DIETS

Vegetarian diets are gaining in popularity for people and dogs. It has become fairly common to find vegetarian dog food available in many pet supplies shops. Until recently, it was usually manufactured in dried form – either flaked or pelleted – but canned vegetarian food is now more widely available.

You may think that it would be easy to prepare vegetarian food for your dog yourself. However, unless you are fairly knowledgeable, you could have considerable difficulty in achieving the correct balance of nutrients.

As a rule, dogs like vegetables, but they are naturally omnivores – in other words, a wild dog eats meat as well as vegetables to survive. A pet dog will always eat meat if it can find some and will not 'choose' a vegetarian diet.

If you are vegetarian and wish to avoid feeding meat to your dog, it is best to start with a young puppy. An older dog will not easily adapt its eating habits. Occasionally, a veterinarian may advise a vegetarian diet for a variety of reasons, including an intolerance of meat, intestinal disorders and obesity.

TYPES OF FOOD

Complete pelleted

Complete pelleted

Canned

Mixer meal

Semi-moist 'sausage'

Biscuits

Vacuum-packed foods

Food marketed as being especially for the smaller breeds of dog is sold in vacuum-packed containers. It is available in quite a wide range of 'recipes' and most dogs – large or small breeds – like it. However, it is fairly expensive and can prove too rich for some dogs' digestive systems. It is useful as an occasional treat or to tempt the appetite of a dog that has been off its food or has a sore mouth.

Canned Food

This is probably the best-known and most popular form of dog food and is available in a vast range of flavours and textures. Some canned foods provide a complete meal, as they already include cereal and other sources of carbohydrate among their ingredients. Others must be mixed with meal to ensure a correct nutritional balance. If you are feeding your dog on complete canned food, provide the essential 'crunch' factor that helps keep teeth and gums healthy with biscuits and chews. Be careful, however, to make sure that you are not over-feeding with extra biscuits and other titbits.

Unopened cans have a long storage life but must be kept refrigerated and used quickly once they have been opened. However, the food tastes and smells more appetizing – to your dog, if not to you – if it is served at room temperature rather than straight from the refrigerator. Do not leave canned food lying around in the dog's dish for prolonged periods, especially during warm weather, as it will attract flies and other pests.

Dried Food

A wide range of dried protein foods have become available over the last ten years. Although the pelleted varieties look like biscuits, they are actually a complete food. They contain all the nutrients a dog requires, as well as the 'crunch' factor essential for exercising the jaws and keeping the teeth clean. Dried food is extremely convenient to serve, rarely causes stomach upsets and, unlike fresh and moist foods, it can be left down for a long time without deterioration. It keeps well, although not indefinitely, as it will eventually lose its vitamin content. Keep an eye on the 'use by' date.

Dried food in the form of flakes is designed to be mixed with water or gravy. It can be stored for quite a long time in the same way as pelleted dried food, but once it has been mixed up it will go off in the same way as fresh or canned food if left down for prolonged periods.

Dog biscuits are available in a wide range of sizes, shapes and flavours, although they are always savoury and sugar-free. They are useful as an occasional treat or as reward for good behaviour and also help to keep the teeth and gums healthy.

WHAT DOGS DRINK

Although plastic bowls are durable, they are easily tipped over. Earthenware is more stable but can be chipped. Stainless steel is unbreakable and easy to clean.

Make sure that there is always a bowl of fresh water available for your dog. Dogs vary considerably in how much they need to drink each day and, of course, are likely to be thirstier in hot weather or after vigorous exercise. Dogs fed on dried food will require more water than those with a moist diet. If you always fill the bowl to the same level each time, you will quickly become aware if your dog is drinking much less or much more than usual. This can be a sign of ill health.

Most dogs enjoy milk, but it should be given only as a treat. It is a food, rather than a drink and can contribute to obesity (see page 30). It may also cause diarrhoea and skin problems, in which case, it is better avoided. Generally speaking, plain water is best. Never give your dog alcoholic drinks; it can become addicted to alcohol in exactly the same way as humans.

Sausages

While some semi-moist foods are bagged in separate meal-size portions, others are sold in the form of a large, plastic-wrapped 'sausage'. Simply cut off the amount required, cover again and store in the refrigerator or a cool place until required for the next meal.

Semi-moist Food

Packed in sealed bags, these are very clean and convenient. Many dogs love them, but they are probably best kept as an occasional treat as they do not always provide the right nutritional balance and can prove very expensive. They are particularly useful if you are travelling with your dog, as they are easy to open, need no preparation and are not messy.

Mixer Meal

This should not be confused with dried food. The nutritional composition is quite different and mixer meal is not a complete food. As the name implies, it is designed to be mixed in with fresh or canned food to provide both crunchy texture and additional vitamins and minerals.

Scraps and Titbits

Any self-respecting dog will be very enthusiastic about your food. If it is good enough for the family, it is good enough for the dog! Once you start feeding your dog scraps, the habit is not easily broken. A dog that pesters at the family dinner table is a nuisance, but you have only yourself to blame if you have given in previously. Feeding table scraps can also lead to obesity (see page 30). Never allow your dog to lick family plates and dishes. If you do allow the occasional treat, transfer leftovers to the dog's own bowl and serve it in the usual place.

'Junk' food, chocolate and other sweet treats are as bad for dogs as they are for children. Many other pre-packed human snacks are heavily salted and can cause kidney damage. A dog biscuit is a far better and healthier treat.

Bones

Most dogs enjoy chewing on a bone, but it is not essential to the dog's diet. Large knuckle bones are the most suitable, but you should never give a dog poultry bones, which can splinter and become stuck in the mouth or throat. Bones can help to keep the teeth in good condition.

PUPPY FOOD

The importance of good-quality, correctly-balanced puppy food cannot be over-emphasized. There is no quicker way of turning a fine puppy into a weedy looking specimen than to feed it a poor diet.

Your puppy's breeder should have supplied you with a comprehensive diet sheet. Follow it rigorously, at least for the first few weeks to help the puppy settle down. Introduce new foods very gradually and one at a time.

There are no hard-and-fast rules on feeding, but the following is a general guide:

- up to three months – four meals a day
- three to six months – three meals a day
- six to 12 months – two meals a day
- from 12 months onwards – one meal a day.

Do not forget to increase the size of the meals as the puppy grows. This seems common sense, but it is surprising how many people forget! By keeping a close watch on your puppy, you can adjust the quantities of food to match its growth requirements at any stage of its development. For example, if it seems to be getting a little plump, reduce the carbohydrate element slightly. Do not be tempted to overfeed any of the giant breeds .

Puppies, like toddlers, have a tendency to eat all kinds of unsuitable things. This may result in a brief attack of mild diarrhoea, which should not cause you anxiety. If the diarrhoea persists, but the puppy is otherwise lively and apparently well, try reducing the quantity of milk in its diet. If it shows any other symptoms of illness, is listless or the diarrhoea does not clear up quickly, consult your veterinarian.

THE ADULT DOG'S DIET

To ensure that your dog stays fit and healthy as an adult, it is imperative that you feed it sensibly and wisely. There can be no strict rule about how much to feed or how many times a day. The amount of food an individual dog requires is governed by various factors, including the amount of exercise it is given. Generally speaking, you are getting it right if your dog is lively, alert and looks in good physical condition.

One or two meals a day is usually sufficient for an adult dog. A good tip is to feed the dog just before or at the same time as you feed the family. This can help prevent begging for table scraps.

If you have more than one dog, it is often sensible to supervise their mealtime, as an assertive dog can push a younger or weaker dog out of the way. Not only can this result in obesity in the

It is difficult to resist the appeal in a dog's liquid brown eyes as it watches the family eat supper, even when you know quite well that it is being fed a perfectly satisfactory diet. A good way to pre-empt this problem is to feed your dog at more or less the same time as you serve the family's meal.

OBESITY

A fat, overweight dog, unable to enjoy life as nature intended, is surely one of the saddest sights you can see. You can kill a dog with kindness, and by over-feeding you will certainly be shortening your dog's life-span. Heart disease, diabetes and arthritis are all associated with overweight.

Some breeds, such as Retrievers, Labradors, Beagles and Dachshunds, are particularly prone to putting on weight and it has been estimated that over 30 per cent of all dogs in Britain and the United States are overweight.

You should be able to feel, but not see your dog's ribs. If you cannot feel them and its body seems to bulge out as you look along it, the dog is almost certainly overweight. Start to remedy this by cutting out all snacks, biscuits and titbits. Make sure that any children in the family understand why you are doing this. You will probably also need to reduce the overall quantity of food. It can be helpful to give the dog two or three smaller meals during the day, rather than a single one.

If you are unable to get your dog back to its correct weight, your veterinarian will undoubtedly be able to assist. After consultation he or she will prescribe a corrective diet, which must be strictly adhered to and, given time, all should be well.

Stocky breeds can put on too much weight without its being immediately apparent. Keep an eye on food intake.

Greed

Some dogs are genuinely greedy, but all tend to bolt their food. This is because, in the wild, dogs had to hunt for their food and there might be several days between meals. Once prey had been caught, it was safest to tear it apart into bite-size chunks and eat it quickly, in case someone bigger came along and stole it. Centuries of domestication have failed to have any effect on this habit.

bossy dog, but also means that you will be less alert to any early signs of illness if one dog is not eating properly.

If you have a cat as well as a dog, it may be a good idea to feed the cat on a higher surface so that its bowl is out of the dog's reach. Not only will this avoid quarrels and, possibly, a scratched nose, but cat food has too high a protein content for dogs and does not provide the nutritional balance they require.

A fit and healthy dog that has sufficient exercise should have no problem in clearing its food bowl. Any sign of picking at food and being choosy could mean that you are actually over-feeding the dog or giving it too many titbits,

which amounts to the same thing. The solution is easy: cut out titbits completely and reduce the amount of food by half for a couple of days and the appetite should improve.

Beware of manipulation. It does not take a dog long to discover that refusing to eat results in a worried owner producing something more delicious than dog food to tempt the appetite. Be firm about this sort of behaviour. Provide the dog's usual food, leave it long enough to give the dog an opportunity to eat it and, if it does not, take the bowl away. Provide the same type of food for the next meal and repeat the procedure. Your dog will soon return to its proper eating pattern and one or two missed meals will do it no harm.

THE DIET DURING PREGNANCY

A bitch may show little or no sign of being in whelp during the first three weeks of pregnancy, as the puppies grow very slowly at this stage. Consequently, there is no need to increase the quantity of food. In fact, it is quite normal for a bitch to go off her food during this period, so it is of prime importance that you supply quality rather than quantity in her diet.

From four to nine weeks of the pregnancy the puppies grow very quickly, so the intake of food must be increased weekly. During this period it is advisable to feed two to three meals a day and in the ninth week, four meals a day. Some bitches are reluctant to eat during the later stages of pregnancy because of abdominal discomfort, so you may find that your bitch's intake of food varies on a daily basis.

THE ELDERLY DOG'S DIET

As your dog grows into middle age, it will probably take less exercise and its metabolic rate will slow down. There are no hard-and-fast rules about when an individual dog can be considered to be elderly; you know your own pet best.

An 'elderly' dog, whatever its age in years, needs a smaller quantity of food, although this should still be of high quality. It may find fish and poultry easier to digest than red meat and the diet can be enhanced with vegetables if necessary. Dogs that have previously been fed on dried food may now find fresh or canned food easier and it is often better to provide two or three smaller meals each day rather than a single, larger one.

There are many special recipes available for the elderly dog. If you are in any doubt about a suitable diet, consult your veterinarian.

Small dogs

Some miniature breeds have very tiny stomachs and it may be better to feed them twice rather than once a day. Many owners of such breeds feed them in this way throughout the dog's life. In any case, it is usually advisable when they are still young adults only just out of puppyhood.

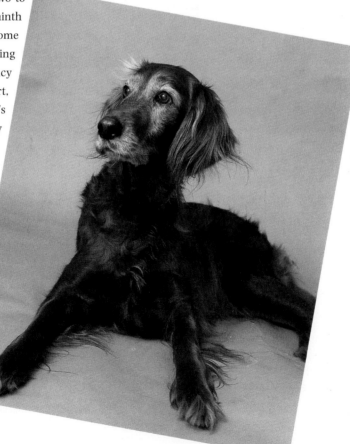

In old age, a dog's digestive system may not work so efficiently. If constipation seems to be a problem, try mixing a little bran into the dog's food.

3

ROUTINE CARE

Some long-coated breeds, such as the Poodle, require regular clipping to prevent their coats becoming unruly. You can do this yourself, but it is easier to take the dog to a professional.

I n the way that a correct diet is essential for maintaining your dog's internal health so it can be said that regular grooming helps to keep your dog looking healthy. You neglect proper grooming at your peril. The coats of long-haired breeds quickly become matted, making subsequent grooming painful.

DAILY GROOMING

Daily grooming helps to maintain the condition and appearance of your dog's coat. It also removes dead hair, which can be a nuisance, especially during moulting. The benefits of this are carried through to the entire household, as the dog will shed less hair on carpets and furniture. Regular attention to long-coated breeds, such as Bichons, that need professional grooming to stop their coats becoming unruly ensures that when they visit the 'hairdresser' the experience will not be too traumatic.

Correct grooming not only removes dirt, dead hair and parasites, but also stimulates the blood supply to the skin. This will certainly make the dog feel better. In addition, if you always closely inspect your dog as part of the daily grooming routine you are likely to notice any minor skin conditions almost as soon as they develop. Obviously, the earlier the diagnosis and treatment, the better it is for your dog.

Approach grooming with a positive outlook. If you consider it boring or a waste of time, your dog will soon sense this, become bored as well and start to fidget. The grooming session will then become even more of a laborious chore. However, your dog will respond to a positive attitude and even start to enjoy the daily session, making things easier for both of you.

The Yorkshire Terrier is a breed that requires very time-consuming grooming if it is not to look scruffy.

Be realistic

Regular grooming to keep your dog's coat in good condition and free from knots, mats and tangles can be a time-consuming business. However, be realistic about your expectations for your family pet and do not imagine that you will be able to match the standards of grooming of dogs that you see in the show ring, unless, of course, you are planning to show your pet. Grooming a dog for showing can become almost a full-time concern, at least with some breeds, who spend much of their lives being bathed, having their coats curled and even wearing a hair-net to prevent lovingly combed ears dangling in their food and water bowls!

GROOMING EQUIPMENT

You will do a better job if you use the correct tools of the trade. Not only will your dog reap the full benefit of your efforts, but you will not be wasting your valuable time and energy.

Be guided in your choice of equipment by the type of coat your dog has. If you are not sure what to use, ask at your local pet shop or check with your veterinarian. They will always be willing to help and advise and can probably sell you the equipment, too.

The larger dog shows usually have trade stands, some of which are devoted solely to grooming products of every possible description.

An old table or bench, providing it is stable, can be a very useful additional piece of 'equipment' when grooming some breeds, to prevent you from developing backache.

It is worth buying good-quality brushes and combs. Cheaper ones tend to disintegrate or their handles break off, making them a false economy.

SHORT-COATED BREEDS
- A good-quality, firm bristle brush
- Rubber grooming mitten
- A coarse comb
- Cotton wool/absorbent cotton
- Chamois leather (optional)

LONG-COATED BREEDS
- Body brush
- Bristle brush
- Long-toothed comb
- Cotton wool/absorbent cotton
- Round-tipped scissors

GROOMING A SHORT-COATED DOG

Grooming a short-coated dog is a relatively quick and easy task. Certainly it takes far less time than grooming long-coated breeds (see pages 36–37). Nevertheless, it should not be neglected: not only is grooming good for the dog (see page 32), but also dogs kept indoors shed hair all year round, so it is in your own interest, too.

1 Using a bristle brush, thoroughly and firmly groom the entire coat, making sure that you brush off any dried mud and debris caught in it. This also helps remove dead hair and skin cells. Brush the underside of the dog gently but firmly, without tickling. (Reverse the order in which you do this if you have a dog that invariably rolls on its back the moment you touch its tummy, especially if you are grooming your dog outdoors.)

2 With the rubber grooming mitten, groom the back, chest and shoulders. Then gently groom both the front and back legs. The grooming mitten is the ideal tool for removing any remaining dead hair and flaking skin cells, as it is stimulating and effective, but not at all scratchy on the dog's skin. Alternatively, use the coarse comb to remove any dead hair and skin, taking care not to scratch.

3 Gently comb the hair around the ears and neck, lifting the dog's chin carefully out of the way. This is a very sensitive area.

4 Gently comb any tail feathering.

5 Using a fresh damp cotton wool/absorbent cotton pad for each eye, gently wipe away any staining and loose hair. Use a third, fresh damp cotton wool/absorbent cotton pad to wipe around the nose.

6 Finish off by polishing the coat to a fine shine with a chamois leather, making sure that you always smooth the coat in the direction in which it grows. This is not essential, but is a professional grooming tip for ensuring a really good glossy coat.

This magnificent Hungarian Vizsla looks superb. The coat is a wonderful shade of russet gold, unique to this aristocratic Gundog, and richly rewards the care and attention of regular, thorough grooming.

GROOMING A LONG-COATED DOG

1 Lift the outer hair and start by brushing the undercoat on the back legs with a body brush. Brush the top coat down with a bristle brush and then comb the coat from the roots to the tips of the hair.

2 Lift the outer hair and brush the undercoat on the front legs with a body brush. Brush the top coat down with a bristle brush and then comb the coat from the roots to the tips of the hair.

3 Supporting the dog's head to keep it out of the way, brush the neck and chest thoroughly.

4 Using a bristle brush, gently but firmly brush along the dog's stomach without tickling it. Make sure that you brush off any dried mud, grass seeds, twigs and other debris.

5 Using the body brush, thoroughly groom the undercoat across the shoulders and along the back. Repeat, using the bristle brush, to groom the dog's top coat.

6 Gently comb the hair around the ears and face. Remember that this is a very sensitive area. Take care not to catch and tug at any tangles (see opposite).

7 Gently comb the tail feathering and any feathers on the backs of the legs, taking care not to tug at any tangles (see opposite).

8 Using a fresh, damp cotton wool/absorbent cotton pad for each eye, gently wipe away any staining and loose hair. Use a third damp cotton wool/absorbent cotton pad to wipe gently around the nose.

Brush the undercoat thoroughly but gently to remove any dirt, debris and tangles.

TANGLES

Even with regular grooming, long-coated dogs may still get tangles, especially after romping in the underbrush on a country walk. Never try to pull out any tangles or knots in the coat, as this can be extremely painful for the dog. Instead, try to split the knot down as small as possible and then remove the pieces of tangled hair.

Use round-tipped scissors to cut the tangle only as a last resort, taking great care not to cut too close to the skin.

WEEKLY GROOMING

Nails or claws should be checked weekly. Correct exercise, such as walking along streets, usually keeps claws filed down. Remember to check the dew claws if they have not already been removed by a veterinarian shortly after birth (they are vestigial and completely functionless). Roughly equivalent in position to human thumbs, they are located slightly above the paws on the inside of either the front or the back legs. These claws do not come into contact with the ground, so

Below left: Supporting the dog's head with your other hand, brush the neck and chest.

Below: Gently comb around the ears and face, taking care not to tug at any tangles.

they tend to grow quite rapidly. In some cases, if left unchecked, they can grow almost into a circle, sometimes piercing the skin and causing unnecessary suffering.

Check the paws for grit and seeds that may have become trapped in between the toes or pads. Remove gently without probing. If a foreign object is lodged between the pads and you cannot easily remove it, consult your veterinarian. Trim any excess fur that has not been worn down with regular exercise, using round-tipped scissors. Be very careful not to cut the skin.

Teeth also need a weekly check. Any blackening or discolouration may require veterinary attention. Remove small tartar deposits with a cotton bud/tip dipped in tooth powder. To be totally up to date, you can invest in your dog's own personal toothbrush and special canine toothpaste!

Check the eyes for excessive tear formation or discharge and the ears for smell, excessive wax and seeds, especially in drop-eared breeds. Never probe into parts of the ear that you cannot see – you could very easily inflict untold damage and pain on your dog. If you think there might be a foreign object or some other problem but are not quite sure what to do, consult your veterinarian.

Plaque deposits can build up on a dog's teeth and if they are not removed regularly, will result in decay.

BATHING

There are no rules about how often you should bath your dog. With the correct diet and proper grooming, it may not really ever need a bath. However, occasionally, a bath may be required for one of two reasons.

- Your veterinarian prescribes one because your dog is suffering from one of the many skin ailments that can affect it. He or she will prescribe an insecticidal or germicidal shampoo, specifically formulated to treat your dog's particular condition.

- Your family prescribes one. Just occasionally, your dog will get it into its head that the best place to play while out on a walk is the dirtiest, smelliest piece of ground or puddle that it can find. Rolling in a cow pat, fox droppings or something equally unsavoury also counts as distinctly anti-social behaviour for which there can be only one solution – a bath.

Short-coated dogs may well go through life needing only good grooming and the occasional dry shampoo, whereas long-coated breeds, especially those with shorter legs, will tend to pick up more mud and dirt. Breeds, such as poodles, that require professional grooming to keep them looking neat and tidy will invariably be bathed during this process and so seldom require bathing at home.

Once you have decided that your dog needs a bath, there are a few things to consider before you start.

- Do not bath your dog if it is under five months old.

- Do not bath a bitch in whelp, especially if she is

over three or four weeks pregnant.

• Think long and hard before bathing a very old dog. Maybe a dry shampoo would be more suitable (see page 41).

• Are the facilities adequate?

Unlike a human, a dog will not get out of the shower and towel itself off. The canine method seems to be to run round like a demented firecracker, shaking water everywhere, until it finds a nice dusty or muddy place where it can lie down and start the cycle off again. In other words, with the larger breeds, there could quite possibly be a lot of water sloshing around. This is definitely not a job to be done in your newly decorated bathroom.

It is no good bathing a long-coated dog if the coat is matted. You will only make things more difficult for yourself when you come to dry and comb out the coat. Make sure the dog is well groomed before giving the bath and then you can be sure that the shampoo you are using is fully able to do its job. This is even more important if you are using one prescribed by your veterinarian.

Finally, a useful tip is to put a non-slip rubber mat in the bottom of the bath or sink. This will help your dog feel more secure and will minimize the amount of water splashed about.

This dog's sheer 'joie de vivre' following its bath is probably best appreciated through a closed window.

Below: A non-slip mat in the bottom of the sink or bath will reduce the amount of splashing and reassure your dog so that it feels more secure. Nevertheless, even small breeds can redistribute quite a lot of water, so it is sensible to protect your clothes before lifting your dog into the sink or bath.

Below right: Work the shampoo well into the coat before rinsing thoroughly with tepid water.

Bathing with Water

1 Ensure that the water is no more than just warm. Lift the dog into the bath or sink and wet thoroughly all over.

2 Pour a little shampoo into your hand and rub it well into the coat, taking care to protect the sensitive areas, such as under the tail, the sheath, the eyes, the ears and the nose.

3 When you are satisfied that the dog is completely washed, rinse thoroughly in clean, lukewarm water to remove all traces of shampoo.

4 As soon as you finish bathing the dog, its natural reaction will be to shake itself. This is fine if you are working outdoors, as it gets rid of a lot of water from the coat. Vigorously rub the dog to remove most of the moisture; you will need several towels to do this.

5 Finish off the drying process with a hairdryer or exercise outdoors. Whichever method you choose, do not allow the dog to become chilled or to stay in a draught while it is still wet. Once they are completely dry, the longer-coated breeds will need combing out (see page 36).

Cleaning with a Dry Shampoo

Dogs can also be 'dry cleaned' with dry shampoo to tidy up their appearance when a bath is not practicable. This is also a good method for elderly dogs, who may find the effort of a bath too much.

1 Sprinkle the powder over the dog's coat, rubbing it well in to absorb grease and dirt. Leave for the time specified by the manufacturer.

2 Brush out the coat, removing all traces of powder and groom the dog thoroughly (see pages 35 and 36).

INOCULATIONS

Routine inoculations are among the most important precautions you can take to safeguard your dog's health. Very young puppies gain immunity from the major infectious canine diseases from the antibodies in their mother's milk. By about eight weeks, after they have been weaned, they must have a course of vaccinations – sometimes two, sometimes three. Be guided by your veterinarian. In North America and most of Europe, rabies vaccination is mandatory. Puppies are usually vaccinated at nine weeks and one year and regular boosters are required. Dog owners in countries where rabies is endemic should consult their veterinarians.

The veterinarian provides a certificate which shows what diseases your dog has been protected against and, most importantly, when you should return for booster vaccinations. This is normally an annual event and it is vital that you remember to do it. For one thing, you are

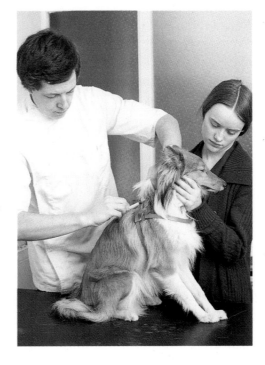

A vital, preventative health-care measure, inoculation is a quick and painless procedure.

putting your dog's health at risk, as immunity does not last a lifetime unless regularly boosted. Secondly, you may be putting your holiday or business trip at risk (see pages 45-46).

The major potentially fatal diseases that can be prevented by vaccination are as follows.

- Leptospirosis – affecting the kidneys and liver
- Hepatitis – affecting the liver
- Parvovirus – can attack the heart in young dogs, while in adult dogs it usually attacks the digestive system
- Distemper – also known as hard pad, attacking the dog's nervous system, sometimes causing fits.

When you take your puppy to the veterinarian for its first inoculations, it will probably also be given a general health-check.

Rabies

Rabies is a fatal disease that can be passed between species, including humans. It is transmitted in the saliva of an infected animal when it bites. Also known as hydrophobia, its main symptom is a fear of water, but foaming at the mouth is also characteristic. Some countries, including Britain, are rabies-free and vaccination against this disease is undertaken only for animals leaving the country. In these circumstances, consult your veterinarian. In countries where rabies is endemic, vaccination of all domestic pets is usually a legal requirement.

PARASITES

The word 'parasite' can conjure up a frightening image. However, adhering to a regular grooming routine and common sense will minimize any problems.

External Parasites

Fleas: The best-known and commonest external parasites are fleas. The first signs that your pet has 'visitors' include scratching and itching. If you part your dog's coat, especially near the head, and you see minute black specks – flea dirt – you need to take action (see opposite).

Lice: Unlike fleas, lice cannot live off the animal and so are easier to treat. Once again telltale signs are lots of itching and scratching. They are easily dealt with using an insecticidal shampoo (see pages 38–40).

Ticks: are often found on dogs that have been

Persistent scratching is usually a sign of flea infestation. Treat your dog to get rid of these unwelcome visitors which are a nuisance in themselves and which can also set up an allergic reaction, causing more itching.

exercised in bracken. They are tiny when they first land on the dog, but bite into its skin and become engorged with blood until they eventually drop off. Obviously it is best to remove them as soon as they are found, but do make sure the whole of the tick comes away. It is very easy to leave part of the head buried in the dog's flesh, which can then develop into an infection requiring treatment. Ticks are rarely a problem for the urban dog.

Internal Parasites

Internal parasites are all known as worms and the importance of regular, effective worming for your dog cannot be over-emphasized. Four types of worms can affect your dog. Fortunately, two of these, whipworm and hookworm, are seldom seen and are easily treated.

Roundworms: These are fairly common, but are also easily treated. They are frequently seen in very young puppies, as they may be passed on from the mother. Your veterinarian may, therefore, recommend worming at two-weekly intervals until the puppy is clear and then at three to six monthly intervals throughout the dog's adult life. With severe infestations, a puppy may sometimes vomit roundworms. In this case, the symptoms are obvious and you should commence treatment as soon as possible.

Tapeworms: The other common type of worm is the tape worm. It can sometimes be seen in faeces, having the appearance of cucumber seeds.

In all cases of worms you should consult your veterinarian, who will be able to advise on the necessary treatment, usually a course of tablets.

Treating your Dog for Fleas

There are many proprietary treatments readily available from your local pet shop or through your veterinarian.

Powder: This is sprinkled over the dog's coat, rubbed in and then left for a specified time before being thoroughly brushed out. This is a fairly inexpensive form of treatment and provides limited immunity from further infestation. Some brands are far more effective than others. It may be unpleasant for both you and your dog as fine powder can irritate the eyes and nasal passages. Most dogs dislike this treatment and it can, therefore, be quite a messy procedure. The dog should not lick its coat while powdered. It is sensible to wear rubber or plastic gloves when applying flea powder and you should wash your hands thoroughly afterwards.

Spray: A liquid preparation is sprayed on the coat, rubbed in and left to dry. Some sprays are in the form of aerosols and others are pump action. Most dogs dislike the hiss of aerosols. Using a pump action spray is slightly slower but does allow more control so that you can ensure the entire body has been treated. Sprays tend to be more expensive but are usually very effective and provide longer immunity from re-infestation. The most effective sprays are available only from veterinarians. It is sensible to wear rubber or plastic gloves when applying flea spray and you should also wash your hands thoroughly afterwards.

Insecticidal shampoo: Formulated to kill external parasites, this treatment can be combined with bathing your dog (see pages 38–40). Many different brands are available and

your veterinarian may prescribe insecticidal shampoo for serious infestation.

Systemic treatments: This is a recently developed form of treatment, available from your veterinarian. It first became available for external application only. The dose varies depending on the size of the dog; consult your veterinarian. The liquid is squeezed onto the back of the dog's neck between the shoulders, that is, a place where it cannot lick. It must be handled with extreme care: you should wear rubber or plastic gloves and not stroke or cuddle your dog for eight to 12 hours after application. Once the liquid has been absorbed into the lymph system, it is completely harmless – except to fleas, which it kills.

A systemic form of treatment is now available for internal use. The preparation, which is harmless to dogs, is taken internally and, once in the dog's system, prevents fleas from breeding, rather than killing them outright.

Flea sprays should be applied liberally to all areas of the dog's coat, taking especial care with thickly furred parts, such as around the neck. Protect the dog's eyes and nose.

Warning

Always follow the manufacturer's instructions when using these preparations. Do not mix different kinds of treatment, with the exception of the two systemic treatments which work most effectively when used together.

A useful tip is never to treat the dog without treating its bedding at the same time or you will just be wasting time.

This means exactly what it says: clean up after your dog. Many towns and cities across the country now have laws requiring you to ensure that your dog does not foul in a public place, but if it does, you should remove the offending article.

Dog faeces are smelly and unpleasant, particularly for mothers with buggies/strollers, children with bicycles and pedestrians in general. Not only do irresponsible people who fail to poop scoop gain a bad name for all dog owners, they place young children at serious risk. Dog faeces sometimes carry the toxocara roundworm which, if it enters a child's bloodstream, can cause blindness. Fortunately, this is rare, but surely it is enough reason to behave responsibly? The simple equipment required – plastic bag or cardboard container – is available either through your local pet shop or your veterinarian.

Warning

The safety features of properly installed, modern household wiring will probably ensure that a puppy chewing through cables and flexes does not electrocute itself. However, trailing flexes can still present a danger because they can catch in the feet of playing pups with the result that appliances, such as televisions, answering machines, telephones and home computers can come crashing down. As well as this causing damage to expensive equipment, it could also injure or kill a young dog.

COMMON HOUSEHOLD HAZARDS

With the inquisitive nature of puppies ordinary things around the home may become sources of danger to the dog or annoyance to you. The following is a list of the commonest hazards to watch out for, but you should keep as alert about all aspects of a puppy's safety – and later, that of your dog – as you would for a toddler's.

• Electric cables and flexes – The awful consequences of your puppy's chewing through a live wire do not bear thinking about. Switch off any electrical appliances that are not in use, keep cables and flexes out of the way and inspect them regularly.

• Stairs – A young puppy should not be trying to use them anyway. Keep an eye on where your puppy is and what it is doing. If you can arrange a secure barrier on the stairs, rather like a child's safety gate, so much the better.

• Thread ties – Ties for bin sacks, ring pulls and plastic ring packaging from multi-pack cans should never be left around where a puppy might ingest them.

• Bones – Investigating kitchen waste is a puppy's idea of heaven. Securely wrap poultry and fish bones and any others that might splinter if chewed.

• Household cleaners – Make sure that disinfectant, bleach, detergent and any chemicals – and their containers – are inaccessible.

Although most dogs are good and often enthusiastic swimmers, you should take care with garden ponds. The tough, sinewy underwater stems of many pond plants can trap unwary paws. Even an adult dog may struggle to the point of exhaustion and drown.

- Sewing and knitting materials – Wool, embroidery threads and reels of sewing cotton pose almost as much threat to a puppy's well-being as such obvious hazards as pins and needles.
- Stationery – Make sure you pick up any dropped items, such as elastic bands, paper clips and map pins, all of which can cause internal damage if ingested.
- House plants – Check that no poisonous plants are within reach.
- Shoes and clothes – Items left lying around are often far too tempting. It can take less than ten minutes of determined chewing to turn a pair of Gucci loafers into a rubbish heap. This is good for neither you nor your puppy.
- Garden or backyard – Is it is secure? You certainly do not need your puppy to disappear into your neighbour's garden and start to play 'chase the cat 'or 'let's dig a flowerbed'. Even more dangerous is the possibility of its managing to get out onto the street. Check fences and repair them if necessary. Cover gaps in gates with wire mesh to prevent a small body wriggling through or burrowing underneath.
- Shed or garage – Keep chemicals, such as slug bait, lawn fertilizer, weedkiller and anti-freeze, out of the puppy's reach.
- Plants – Some common garden plants and shrubs are poisonous.
- Ponds – Keep them covered. Puppies can drown.

For advice on safety in the street and in cars, see pages 66–67.

KENNELS AND SITTERS

When you come to take a well-earned break, you will have to find a temporary home or minder for your pet. Modern boarding kennels are subject to thorough inspection by licensing authorities. Nevertheless, you should never leave your dog in kennels that you have not personally checked out. Always telephone beforehand to establish business hours, charges and availability, but arrive unannounced to inspect the kennels.

You should principally be looking for the following points.

- Are the kennels clean, light and airy?
- Are the sleeping quarters clean and draught-free?
- Are there ample facilities for daily exercise?
- Are the dog's quarters secure, preferably with a double door?
- How often and thoroughly are the dogs

Kennels vary in price and the quality of the care they provide, from fairly basic 'bed-and-breakfast' to a five-star luxury suite. At the very least, they must be hygienic, draught-free, secure and provide adequate routine care and exercise.

Watch points for dog sitters

- Follow up references from any professionals to whom you are trusting your beloved pet and your home.
- Arrange for your dog sitter to arrive the day before you go away so that you have adequate time to explain the routine and where everything is kept.
- Always leave a note of where you can be contacted and your veterinarian's name, address and telephone number.

groomed? This is especially important if you have a long-coated dog.

- Is there a local veterinarian on 24-hour call?
- Are special diets catered for and are there any additional charges for this facility?
- Do all dogs boarded at the kennels have to be vaccinated? (They should be.)
- Do the kennels require all boarders to be vaccinated against kennel cough? This is a highly infectious cough which, if encountered, is seldom fatal but can be extremely distressing.

An increasingly popular alternative to kennels is to use a house sitting service. These are organizations which, for a fee, can provide someone to live in and take care of your house while you are on holiday. As with the kennels, you need to research thoroughly to establish availability, charges and the willingness and ability of the sitter to look after your dog as well as your house. The sitter must visit you before you go away in order to establish your pet's routine and to find out where everything is kept.

As well as supplying routine care, an experienced dog sitter, while no substitute for your company, provides your dog with the warmth of a human friend in the reassuring security of its own home during your absence.

SPAYING AND CASTRATION

This topic is rife with 'old wives' tales' and it seems that everyone, apart from your veterinarian, will give you a completely different, usually ill-informed view.

First of all, deciding whether your bitch should be spayed or your dog should be castrated is strictly your concern and has nothing to do with whether it would be 'good' or 'bad' for the animal. It is a very common fallacy to think that having a litter will improve a bitch or be 'fair' to her. It makes no difference to her at all and creates a lot of hard work for you. Having a bitch spayed means that you do not have to confine her to the house every time she comes into season, which will probably be twice a year and for up to three weeks at a time (see opposite).

Despite what some people say, a castrated dog will never know what he is missing. It is foolish to ascribe human thoughts and emotions to animals. In the past, spaying bitches tended to be the generally accepted surgery, but castration is now widely performed. Besides ensuring that your dog is not responsible for the birth of any more unwanted puppies, it can be helpful in tackling some behavioural problems, such as aggression, wandering and anti-social (from the human point of view) scent marking. Should you decide that castration is the preferred course of action, talk to your veterinarian who will be only too happy to give you sensible advice and reassurance.

If, after due thought, you still feel that a litter would enrich both your lives, see the following chapter on breeding (pages 48–55).

BITCHES IN SEASON

Your puppy bitch may start to attain sexual maturity from as early as six months of age, when she may have her first season. This is also sometimes known as coming 'on heat'. As a general rule, subsequent seasons last on average about three weeks and can occur as frequently as every four months, but are more likely to occur at six monthly intervals. During this time, there will be a light bloodstained discharge and the bitch's scent will attract male dogs wherever she goes.

One golden rule if your bitch is in season and you do not want her to have puppies: do not let her mix with male dogs. This may mean keeping her confined indoors. If you take her for her daily romp in the park, she will attract the attention of every male dog within a two-mile radius, who will then follow you home, whine, whimper and generally try to find a way in. This is not good for neighbourhood relations and risks an 'accident'.

Modern veterinary science has produced a couple of methods of either delaying or disguising a season, one of which involves a course of injections and the other a course of tablets. Your veterinarian will be happy to provide further information and advise on their suitability for your bitch.

Sprays that are designed to disguise the scent of a bitch in season are available, but are not always effective. An alternative method is to spray the bitch with diluted lavender oil. Always use pure essential oil, diluted with water and applied with a pump action spray. Your veterinarian may also be able to advise on homeopathic methods.

This English Setter bitch gazes forlornly through the kitchen window, unable to understand why she has been confined to a dog-run in the garden while her brother has the freedom of the house and is still taken out for their usual routine walks.

4

BREEDING

All your hard work and effort in rearing your puppy has come to fruition, you now have a good-looking, adult bitch and, perhaps like many people, you are thinking 'Let's let her have a litter. It will do her good and we'll make lots of money from selling the puppies.' You are wrong! There is absolutely no evidence to support either of these contentions. Breeding and rearing puppies should always be done for love not financial gain. Even so, there are many things to take into consideration before you commit your bitch to having a litter.

Little can compare with the sense of satisfaction you will feel in rearing the puppies bred from your own much-loved bitch.

- Is your dog fit and healthy?
- Is she strong enough to undergo the rigours of pregnancy?
- Are you confident in your ability to see your dog through this experience?
- Is there a ready market for puppies of your breed?
- Do you have any firm bookings for your puppies?

As a responsible dog owner you must consider the fact that every year hundreds of dogs are dumped because they are unwanted. Unless you are absolutely confident in your ability to find permanent homes for all of the puppies, you should not even begin to consider the idea.

If you are totally committed and determined to go ahead – good luck. Allowing for a little good fortune, you can look forward to the immense pleasure of owning a dog that you have bred and of which you can be justifiably proud.

The Stud Dog

You may be asked if you would allow your dog to be used at stud. Having considered all the pros and cons previously mentioned, you also have to decide if the bitch is suitable. If you decide to go ahead, you have to reach an agreement over any fee that you may wish to charge and it is advisable to record this in writing, ensuring that both parties have a copy.

Care of the stud dog does not require any more than a normal sensible diet with plenty of exercise to keep him in the peak of condition.

PREGNANCY AND BIRTH

You need to plan well in advance and to select a suitable stud dog. It is a good idea to worm your bitch before she is mated to minimize the chances of her passing worms onto her puppies. Another sensible precaution before the mating is to have her vaccinated, so that she passes on the maximum maternal antibodies to her puppies.

The gestation period for a bitch is 63 days, but this can vary by a couple of days either way. During this time, she requires normal care and attention, but as she becomes heavier, restrict her exercise and exclude any rough-and-tumble with children. There is no need to start feeding extra food until about the fourth week of the pregnancy, as she will only get fat (see page 31).

As the day approaches, she may start to seek out a quiet, dark place, where she can dig and make a 'nest'. Do not allow her to do this. Instead, encourage her to 'nest' in the whelping box. The box, which you can make yourself, should have plenty of room so that the bitch can stretch out comfortably. The sides should be high enough to contain the puppies, but low enough to allow their mother to jump out with ease. If she is introduced to a whelping box quite early in the pregnancy, she will probably be happy to use it as a 'nest'.

Watch her closely during the last week of pregnancy, as she may try to hide in an

False pregnancy

Sometimes a non-pregnant bitch may appear to be pregnant, usually about nine weeks after her last season. This false or pseudo-pregnancy lasts about two months, during which she shows all the signs of a genuine pregnancy, including an increase in weight and the production of milk. The symptoms are often completely convincing and even experienced breeders have sometimes been misled. False pregnancy is probably due to a hormonal imbalance and tends to recur. It may lead to a more serious uterine condition. You should always consult your veterinarian, who may recommend spaying.

CANINE MATING

Mating begins with a period of flirting and then the dog mounts the bitch. Clasping her behind the ribs with his forelegs enables him to penetrate her. Once he has ejaculated, he needs to turn, ending up in the position illustrated here. To do this, he lifts one foreleg over the bitch's back, so that both forelegs are on the same side of the bitch. Then he lifts the corresponding hindleg gently over her hindquarters. The two are now standing back to back and may remain in this position from ten minutes to one hour.

Mixed litters

More than one dog can mate with a bitch during a season, so if this pregnancy was unplanned, it is possible she may bear a mixed litter, that is puppies sired by different dogs. If a mis-mating has occurred, your veterinarian can give your bitch an injection that will prevent her having puppies. Take her to your veterinarian as soon as possible after the mating, preferably within 36 hours. The popular 'old wives' tale' that a pedigree bitch is ruined for future breeding if she bears a litter of non-pedigree puppies has no scientific foundation.

THE ANATOMY OF A PREGNANT DOG

The canine uterus has two 'horns', narrowing towards the ovaries.

inaccessible place. However, the only true indication that whelping is imminent is a fall in her temperature to below 37.8°C/100°F. Your role during the actual whelping is to stand by in case you are needed.

When the first puppy is born, the bitch will tear the amniotic sac surrounding it and start to lick the newborn. Licking stimulates the puppy as well as cleans it. Check that the puppy's mouth is clear and, if necessary, rub its chest with a fairly rough towel to help get it breathing.

The mother will bite through the umbilical cord and may eat the afterbirth. This provides additional nutrients, but do not worry if she does not eat them all. It is important that you see an afterbirth for every puppy she delivers, as a retained placenta can cause an infection.

Help the puppy to latch onto a teat so that it can feed. Once mother and puppy are settled, clean the box, put down some fresh newspaper and wait for the next puppy.

Puppies are born sightless, deaf and completely helpless. They are totally dependent on their mother.

PREPARING FOR THE BIRTH

There are several things you must organize well in advance and have available when the day comes.

- Warn your veterinarian as early as possible of the impending birth. He or she will appreciate this far more than being called on for emergency help unexpectedly. In fact, after taking into account all the factors, the veterinarian may even recommend that the bitch stays with him or her for the duration of the birth.
- You will need lots of old newspapers to put on the floor of the whelping box.
- Prepare a cardboard box containing a well-covered hot water bottle. As the bitch becomes restless and prepares for the next arrival, place the puppies in the box, where they will be perfectly comfortable and out of the mother's way.
- Have a few clean towels handy for drying newborn puppies, if necessary. If they arrive in quick succession, the bitch may not have time to clean them herself, or if she is becoming exhausted, she may simply not have the energy.
- Sterilize a pair of round-tipped scissors and some strong thread in boiling water in case you have to cut and tie the umbilical cord.
- Make sure the telephone is nearby in case you need to call for veterinary assistance.

PROBLEMS DURING AND AFTER WHELPING

- If the bitch has gone into labour and has been seen to be having contractions, you must call your veterinarian if nothing has happened after 30 minutes or she appears to be settling down again. This may indicate a wrongly presented puppy or the bitch may have become exhausted and unable to push.
- Sometimes there may be a deformed puppy in the litter. Remove it from the litter as soon as possible.
- Eclampsia, also known as milk fever, requires prompt attention from the veterinarian. Its onset may be very sudden. The symptoms are drowsiness or severe unsteadiness caused by calcium deficiency. It is cured quite quickly by a calcium injection.
- Some breeds, such as the Irish Setter, tend to have large litters. In this case, labour may be quite prolonged and the bitch may have little opportunity to rest between births. She can become exhausted and unable to push. Seek veterinary assistance.
- Large-headed breeds, such as the Bulldog, are often more safely delivered by Caesarean section.
- Reluctance to feed the puppies may be caused by mastitis, an infection of the teat which is extremely serious and requires veterinary treatment. It may also be caused by an excess of milk, making the bitch feel uncomfortable. Expressing some milk by hand, thus relieving the pressure, usually resolves the problem.

Foster feeding

If a puppy is orphaned, the mother rejects it or she is unable to feed it, you will have to take over. Feeding bottles and puppy milk formula are available from veterinarians and pet stores. Do not use cow's milk or human formula, both of which have the wrong balance of nutrients. You will have to feed at two-hourly intervals, day and night, to begin with, gradually reducing the number of feeds as the puppy grows. Sterilize all the equipment, including the measuring scoop. This is important, as the puppy will not be receiving natural antibodies from its mother. Prepare the formula according to the manufacturer's instructions and warm to blood heat just before feeding. Either prepare the feed for the next 24 hours and store in the refrigerator until needed or mix the formula freshly each time. After each feed, wipe the puppy's mouth and anal area with separate cotton wool/absorbent cotton pads moistened with warm water to stimulate urination and bowel movement.

NEWBORN PUPPIES

Once the puppies are settled, the first thing to do is to record their weights. Thereafter a weekly weighing programme is essential to ensure that the litter is growing evenly and that they are all gaining weight.

Keep the puppies warm in a draught-free place. An infra-red lamp is ideal for this purpose. There are

For the first few weeks, the puppies will spend most of their time snuggled cosily together in the whelping box when they are not feeding. Their mother takes care of all their needs.

two types: one which gives out light and heat and one which radiates heat only. Use only the second type. Correctly positioned, it will keep the puppies warm and comfortable.

Cleanliness is of prime importance. Very young puppies are extremely susceptible to infection of any sort, so take care that you do not transmit any bugs to them. Always wash your hands thoroughly before you attend to them. It is perfectly natural for the mother to clean up after the puppies, so you should be making your contribution by changing the bedding when it becomes soiled.

The First Weeks

Puppies are both sightless and deaf when born. The eyes start to open when they are about ten days old and they are able to hear at approximately three weeks. Movement around the whelping box, if a little unsteady, also begins to take place about this time. For at least the first three weeks of their life, the mother will care totally for her brood, both cleaning and feeding them.

With such a demand on the mother's resources, it is of great importance that you make sure you are providing her with enough to eat and drink (see page 31).

GROWING PUPPIES

Start to wean the puppies from about three weeks of age. The first bowl of milk you give them is very entertaining. They do not know what to do with it and paddle it everywhere. Once they have got the idea, they will quickly become more than ready to try lapping at semi-solid foods.

Make sure that all the puppies are feeding equally, even if this means allowing the smaller, weaker ones to eat separately. Over the course of the next two to three weeks, you should be trying to get the litter away from feeding from their mother. At first, she will not be keen on leaving them, but with your encouragement, she will soon start to feel more comfortable about this. By week five, the puppies should very nearly be independent of their mother. She should really be going into the whelping box only to clean up behind her brood, with the very occasional attempt to feed them.

While she is still feeding her litter make sure she does not become too red and sore around her teats. Puppies' claws grow very quickly and are really sharp. Clip the claws if necessary. If you do not feel confident, ask an experienced friend or veterinarian to show you how to do it.

By about six weeks, the litter should be feeding on six meals a day, with the diet evenly split between milky foods and all kinds of meat. Get them used to a variety of flavours to prevent them being faddy and difficult as adults. The food you supply should be of the highest quality. As the saying goes, you only get back what you put in to start with. A vitamin or mineral supplement can be a useful addition to the diet

CLIPPING YOUR PUPPY'S CLAWS

• Gently squeeze the puppy's paw to expose the maximum area of claw.
• Examine the claw; you should be able to see that there is a cortex or 'quick' near to the paw. This is living material that contains the blood supply, while the tip is composed of dead cells.
• Using nail clippers or special claw clippers, cut off the sharp tip of the claw. Do not cut through the quick or you will hurt the dog.

and your veterinarian will advise you on this.

The puppies start to cut their first teeth around this time. A pair of old socks tied together in a big knot makes a useful plaything and something for them to chew on. Indeed, play is now an important activity. You will find that you have several bundles of fur that fly around the whelping box, play-fighting and generally enjoying their new life. Then suddenly they fall into a deep sleep, only to wake up and demand food. This period of growth, from five to about eight weeks of age, is extremely interesting to observe as you see the individual characters begin to develop. In fact, if you are not careful, you can find that you have lost most of your day puppy-watching!

Warning

Once the puppies are fully weaned, they will no longer be receiving the antibodies from their mother's milk, which give them immunity to various infections. From this time until they have been inoculated, they are vulnerable to infection. Do not relax your vigilance and make sure that visitors are equally scrupulous. Certainly, do not allow anyone to bring other dogs into your home.

Once your puppies are beginning to grow up, you will find their antics a constant, if sometimes messy, source of delight.

FINDING HOMES

In a perfect world, it should not be necessary to write about this at all, as all the puppies would have been sold before they were even born. This is not always possible, but you should, at least, have had some enquiries about a possible litter before you even mated your bitch so that just a few puppies are left to sell at this stage.

There is no best place to advertise, so spread your news as widely as possible. Local newspapers are good places to start and if your veterinarian will allow it, a card on his or her notice board can sometimes promote a few enquiries. If you have joined the dog showing fraternity, you are likely to receive quite a few telephone calls, especially if you have already had some success in the show ring. The following list is a helpful reminder.

- Let your friends know that your dog has had puppies and that you are seeking homes for them.
- Let the breed club secretary know, so that the puppies can be listed.
- Advertise in local newspapers and specialist magazines.
- Ask your veterinarian if you can put a notice on his or her board.

Do not allow puppies to go to new homes until they are least seven or eight weeks old, by which time they will be fully weaned and wormed. For your part, you will be looking for people that you feel can continue to look after the puppy and care for it to the same standards you have kept up since its birth. You, as the breeder, have to supply a puppy that is in tip-top condition. Interview prospective owners to ensure that they will be providing the permanent loving care that your puppies deserve. Watch out for the following points.

- Always ask what their working arrangements are and whether the dog will be left on its own during the day and for how long.
- Ask if they have any other pets.
- Ask if they have children and, if so, what age. If the children are very young and have never owned a dog before, it may be better for them to wait until they are older and ready to accept the great responsibility of caring pet ownership.
- Ask if they have any intention of breeding; there are any number of greedy and very unscrupulous 'puppy farms' around.

- Never sell the whole litter to one buyer. This often means that they are destined for some disreputable place, such as a research laboratory.
- Prepare a diet sheet and a record of any vaccinations and worming treatments the puppy may have had. It is sensible to recommend that the new owner takes the puppy for an examination by his or her own veterinarian as soon as practicable.

Finally, do not forget to provide an efficient, and friendly 'after-sales service'. Be prepared to provide lots of advice, help and encouragement to the new owners.

Watch points

- Trust your instincts. You will usually have a 'gut' reaction to prospective purchasers.
- Do not allow yourself to be pressurized. If a would-be purchaser seems unsuitable, for any reason, be firm in your refusal to sell your puppy.
- Keep a record of purchasers' addresses, so that you can follow up your puppies' progress for the first few weeks in their new home.

Advise prospective owners of the size and personality they can expect when the puppy grows up. This cute little Cocker Spaniel will grow to a maximum height of 40 cm/15¾ inches and is likely to become an ideal family pet because of its affectionate cheerful nature and liking for children.

5

THE SOCIAL DOG

The key to successful dog training is to make full use of your dog's instinctive desire to please you.

After the first few weeks when you and your puppy have been getting to know each other, it is time to start thinking about the next steps forward. There may be any number of reasons for people to buy a puppy: to be a gundog, a working guard, to compete in obedience competitions or just to be a well-behaved pet. Whatever your particular reason, it should go without saying that you will *both* need training in order to fulfil your joint potential. More complex training tends to be ongoing and is best left to specialists, but this chapter shows you ways of teaching your dog some simple obedience commands. Learning these will result in a dog that respects you as the boss and is a pleasure to own.

Early training for puppies includes both house training and teaching it how to behave when on a lead. No matter how entertaining and delightful your pet is as a youngster, your pleasure will soon pale if it grows into an unruly adult. Uncontrolled and bad behaviour is tiresome and unappealing. Worse, an undisciplined dog on a lead can cause accidents. It is never too soon to start the training; even wearing a soft collar while still young helps a puppy to adjust to the real thing later. Always remember that training should be treated as an enjoyable part of your relationship and not as a chore to be endured. That way, you will be pleasantly surprised by the skills you have developed and gratified by what you have achieved.

TRAINING

You will probably already have had some thoughts about training when you were considering which breed of dog really interested you in the first place. It is no use choosing a breed just because it looks impressive and because the neighbours have not got one; that is a sure first step on the way to disaster. To take an extreme example, it is highly unlikely that you could manage to train a Bulldog to be a gundog.

Success in training is achieved through a combination of factors, including the dog's responsiveness, your patience and persistence and the frequency of training sessions.

It is imperative that you appreciate the differences between the way people and the way dogs think. Human and canine behaviour patterns are very different. The dog is naturally a pack animal and needs to establish a leader. Compared to people, it is capable of learning only simple commands.

Choosing a Name

The very first thing your puppy must get used to is hearing and recognizing its own name. It helps if you choose a short clear-sounding name with hard consonant- sounds like 't', 'ck' and 'x' at its end, as long, polysyllabic or soft-sounding words are much more difficult for the puppy to learn. Once you have settled on a name, you should never change it and should use it at every possible opportunity.

House Training

Young puppies cannot be expected to stay perfectly clean through the night, so you must be prepared for some accidents at first. Always have a thick layer of old newspaper on the floor and put the puppy on the paper after every meal. Remember to be encouraging if the puppy actually performs!

Constant repetition will soon teach the puppy what the paper is for. Once it has learned this, you can move the newspaper closer to the door and you will soon find that you are opening the door to let the puppy out. If there is an occasional accident, do not be too harsh, as this is likely to undo all the good you have done.

A properly-trained dog that knows it is behaving in a way that pleases you is likely to be well-adjusted and content.

Watch point

If you have had your dog since it was a puppy and brought it up and trained it properly, you are unlikely to encounter problems once it is an adult. However, if you have taken on an adult rescue dog, it may have already acquired all sorts of bad habits or, perhaps, never have been trained at all. The best way of controlling a strong, untrained and persistently unruly dog is with a head collar. This gives you total control without causing the dog any discomfort and it will soon learn to walk to heel and obey all the basic commands.

Lead Training

Before you attempt any form of lead training, the puppy should be completely accustomed to wearing a soft collar, otherwise you will be inflicting a double blow to its confidence. When you first attach a lead it will seem very strange to the puppy. It will probably want to go off exploring and will not understand why it cannot get away from you.

Hold the lead and encourage the puppy to come towards you, maybe using a treat to entice it to move. With repetition the puppy soon learns to overcome its nervousness and starts to enjoy the training.

Once the dog is readily coming to you, you can start to encourage it to walk alongside. Do not let it pull out in front of you; this is a bad habit and must be discouraged right from the start. Once your puppy fully accepts the collar and lead, continue further training using a check chain (see page 60).

Now that you have successfully got your dog moving properly on the lead, you have to teach it

to stop on command. Jerk the check chain backwards, giving the command 'sit' at the same time. Repeat the command, press down firmly on the rear quarters and encourage it to sit. Give lavish praise whenever the dog responds correctly. After all, it is having to listen to you and decide what it is that you want it to do. When you have accomplished the 'sit', release the pressure on the check chain and walk on, giving the command 'heel'. Repeating this sequence several times, once or twice a day, will soon produce a dog that looks forward to going for a walk and is a pleasure to take out.

One further basic command for the dog to learn is to sit and stay. Still on its lead, put the dog in the 'sit' position, turn and face it and give the command 'stay' at the same time as putting your hand in front of its face. If the dog moves, jerk the check chain, just to remind it who is the boss. Once the basic 'stay' is achieved, move a little further away from the dog each time, still using your hand as a visual signal and repeating the 'stay' command as often as necessary.

Right: Jerk the check chain backwards and give the command 'sit'. Repeat the command, while pressing down the hindquarters.

Far right: Put the dog in the 'sit' position, turn to face it and give the command 'stay', while holding your hand in front of its face.

REWARDS AND INCENTIVES

Dogs cannot tell the difference between right and wrong; they simply do what most suits them. It can, therefore, be useful to provide an extra incentive during training in the form of occasional treats. When the dog knows that it receives a special titbit after obeying a command properly, it is in its own interests to continue obeying. You do not have to give it a treat every time, once it has learned the command, but giving one now and again will reinforce the lesson.

It is also in the dog's interests to please you, the pack leader. Lavish praise and encouragement when the dog has done well will make it want to do so again. Equally, when a dog does something wrong, a stern 'no' and your clear disapproval will discourage it from repeating the offence.

This owner and dog provide a classic example of what not to do. While they are having lots of fun racing about in the park, the dog has taken charge and is taking his owner for a walk, rather than the other way round. It might be more of a problem in the street.

Firm principles

Whether you eventually do decide to become more deeply involved in training, it really is an absolute requirement that you teach your dog to respond to your basic commands. A dog that is allowed to behave exactly as it wishes is a danger to itself, its owner and the public at large.

Going to school

Puppy 'playschools' have recently been developed and many people have found them a useful method of starting the process of full socialization and training of their dogs. They are the canine equivalent of nursery schools or kindergartens for children – the education is preliminary, general and gentle, helping the young animal (canine or human) adjust to the standards expected of it as it grows up, punctuated by lots of fun and playing.

TIPS FOR TRAINING

With all types of training, consistency of instructions, frequency of sessions and, above all, endless patience are necessary to achieve the desired result. Training sessions should not need to exceed ten to 15 minutes each time, otherwise the dog will become both bored and confused, which, in turn, will shorten your temper and undermine what you have already achieved .

By the time your puppy is six months old, both you and it should be perfectly capable of carrying out all the basic tasks described previously. If you have been inspired by your joint achievements, you may wish to consider joining one of the local dog training clubs. There you will be able to confirm that you are training your dog properly and find expert help and guidance to help you overcome any problems you may encounter. If you eventually wish to enter the world of competitive obedience trials, there will be plenty of like-minded people to help you move in the right direction.

EXERCISE

A fit dog enjoys both food and exercise. In fact, exercise can be described as the key to a dog's healthy appetite, as it burns off much of the energy supplied by food. It also helps to maintain its interest in life; a dog that is always confined with no freedom becomes fat and poorly conditioned – the canine equivalent of the human couch potato! Boredom, expressed by constant barking, also sets in and all-in-all the dog can become fairly miserable.

Equally, the 'latch key' dog, let out to roam the streets on its own, is a danger to itself, its owner and the general public. A lack of control may cause it to develop anti-social habits, such as scavenging. With no owner to look up to it may even become aggressive. Certainly, it will derive no physical benefit from uncontrolled meandering through the streets.

On the other side of the coin, a dog given regular daily exercise tends to be healthy, alert, well-adjusted, socially acceptable and, in

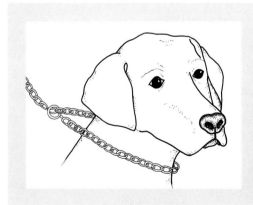

THE CHECK CHAIN

It is important that the check chain is used correctly. Make sure the chain passes over the dog's neck and back underneath; not the other way round. The chain should hang loose around the neck when no pressure is being applied.

The dog will soon learn that if it moves from the correct position when walking alongside you, the chain pulls tight.

general, a pleasure to own.

The term exercise is relative to the breed that you own. Some of the smaller breeds can be adequately exercised in a garden, while larger, more sporting dogs will need free-range running, maybe twice a day, for at least 45 minutes each time. Exercise periods should always be accompanied, if only to ensure the safety of the dog. They also provide an opportunity to continue training and, if that is not enough, the walk will do you good as well!

Exercise Through the Ages

As a puppy grows up and an adult dog ages, its exercise requirements alter. Exercise for puppies under the age of six months should be restricted to walking on the lead and playing in the garden, as over-exertion at this age can hinder physical development. Exercise throughout the dog's prime years, while controlled, should be adequate to ensure maintenance of its physical condition. If the dog settles down for a sleep soon after returning from its walk, it is probably getting about the right amount of exercise. If it comes home still bursting with energy, it is not getting enough.

Swimming is particularly beneficial, but you must remember that the dog should be thoroughly towelled off after a dip, otherwise a chill may result. Also, do make sure that the place where it swims is not polluted, that there are no submerged obstacles that might cause injury and the banks are not so steep that getting out again is a problem.

Teaching your dog to retrieve is also an

excellent way of ensuring that it has plenty of vigorous healthy exercise without your becoming completely exhausted.

In its later years your pet may not be able to take such strenuous exercise and you should adjust accordingly. Quite a good maxim is not too far or too fast. Remember to keep a check on the claws at this time (see pages 37 and 53) as well, because decreased exercise will allow them to grow a little more than you will have been used to when the dog was younger.

However you exercise your dog it should always be a pleasure and never a chore. If you do not enjoy it, neither will your dog, which will make the whole thing seem a bit pointless. Regular daily sessions are a vital part of the relationship between you and your dog – you neglect them at your own risk.

Exercise is vital to your dog's well-being. The needs of different breeds vary dramatically. Small dogs and heavy breeds require no more than about 1.6 km/ 1 mile daily, while working dogs, like this one, many Utility breeds, Hounds, Gundogs and most Terriers will take 16 km/ 10 miles a day literally in their stride.

When a dog is inviting another one to play, the first thing it usually does is 'bow', lowering its forelegs and raising its hindquarters, while looking straight at its potential playmate. This is then followed by a session of jumping about with the tail wagging vigorously. If the other dog then wants to join in, the game generally starts with a good chase and a 'wrestling' match.

PLAY

Play is essential for both exercise and socialization. Through play, puppies learn to mix with each other and with the human part of their pack. In fact, dogs are one of the few animals that continue to play throughout their lives and not just in infancy. Playing with your dog is a vital part of your relationship and reinforces your roles within the pack.

There are many special puppy and dog toys available and plenty more that can be homemade. A ball is a traditional favourite and chasing after one provides plenty of vigorous activity. Make sure the ball is too big to be swallowed and cause choking. Frisbees have recently become very popular and dogs have proved to be immensely skilful in twisting and jumping up to catch them.

In fact, in some places, there are frisbee championships for dogs. Special dog frisbees are available, but any one made of lightweight plastic that will not damage the dog's mouth may be used. Nylon chews, kongs and dumbbells are all popular and help to keep teeth and gums healthy. However, a pair of old socks knotted together also provides endless and completely free amusement. Tug toys, usually made of chew-resistant rubber, are great fun, but should never be used with assertive, 'mouthy' dogs.

It is important that there are rules about play and that all the family understands them. Dogs can become over-excited when playing if the game is not properly controlled. Never allow growling or frenzied barking; stop the game until the dog has calmed down. Play biting is not play at all. Puppies and young dogs will play-fight with each other, but an adult dog should never snap its teeth as part of family fun. Do not allow your dog to run the game. You are the one in charge, who gets out and puts away the toys. A dog that seizes a toy and growls when anyone comes near is showing worrying signs of anti-social behaviour. Equally, however, do not let children or even unthinking adults tease a dog.

Cheap and cheerful, a large ball can provide many hours of amusement for both large and small breeds of dog. A game of canine 'football' is always a treat.

The 'meeting and greeting' ritual undertaken by two dogs – whether meeting for the first or the hundred and first time – is rather like a complicated minuet, with each dog understanding the 'steps' and going through the motions.

MEETING AND GREETING

Since it was first domesticated, the dog, despite being a dominant pack animal in its own right, has readily accepted man as its master and has remained a faithful companion ever since. However, you will be very much mistaken if you think that every dog that you meet will behave exactly as you expect. All dogs – whatever their size – demand respect and never so much as when they encounter someone new.

It is most important that visitors are actually *introduced* to your dog the first time that they come to see you. Your confidence in visibly accepting their presence does much to allay any fears that the dog may have. However, if they are accompanied by their own dog, it is not a good idea for the two animals to meet for the first time where one of them has the advantage of 'home' ground. A walk on neutral territory, such as in the local park, allows both dogs to go through their complicated 'meet and greet' ritual without either of them feeling threatened.

The children in your own family will have learned to treat their dog with proper respect, but this does not automatically apply to their friends. Young visitors should always be supervised. A dog can easily misunderstand boisterous, noisy play and may feel called upon to 'defend' a member of its pack.

AGGRESSION

Breeds originally bred as fighting dogs are not necessarily aggressive towards people, although some, given the chance, will always challenge any other dog they meet. In Britain, some breeds, such as the Pit Bull, are legally obliged to wear a muzzle in public places.

An aggressive dog has either gained the upper hand psychologically over its owner or it has been incorrectly trained (or both). The trick is to make sure that *you* are the leader of the pack and not your dog.

The best time to start eliminating aggression is as soon as it appears. If you have been lucky enough to buy a pair of puppies, you may find

one becoming dominant over the other. The best method for curing this is to pick up the culprit, look it straight in the eye and tell it exactly what you think of it! Of course, the dog will not understand the words you use, but it will certainly take note of the tone of your voice and your body language. The sound of a rolled-up newspaper being banged on a table can also distract the dominant dog just long enough for you to catch its eye; sometimes that is all that is needed to achieve the desired effect.

Physical aggression towards other dogs must be controlled and then eradicated if possible. However, just as some people are overtly aggressive to others, some dogs behave in a similar manner. Such a dog needs an owner to demonstrate great strength of character in order to curb the aggressive streak.

Using the Lead and Check Chain

When you go out, keep a dog with aggressive tendencies on the lead and use the check chain. When you are passing another dog, walk so that you are between the two of them. Do not take a walking stick to drive other dogs away; this is likely only to inflame them. Dragging your dog off every time you see another dog also reinforces bad habits. However, you may find that you can defuse a potential confrontation by sharply calling your dog's name, giving a jerk on the chain and turning round to walk – not scuttle – away from the possible adversary. Should your dog become embroiled in a fight, do not intervene as you risk injury to yourself. Sounding a rape alarm has sometimes proved effective in stopping dog fights.

THINK 'DOG'

Punishment of a dog that has misbehaved should never be physical. You can achieve far more by approaching the dog on a psychological front than you ever will through violence.

A dog naturally tries to please its master and your expression of displeasure will usually be more than enough to make it feel chastised. It is no good, however, chastising the dog *after* the event. It must be carried out at the time, for how else is the dog to understand what it has done wrong?

For example, suppose your dog does not return to your side immediately but only on the second or third time of calling. If you tell it off, the dog's reasoning says, 'Why should I go back there when I only get told off?' Instead, it should be praised.

The secret to an enjoyable and smooth-running relationship is to think 'dog'.

BAD HABITS

- There is very little that will annoy your neighbours more than a dog's incessant barking, particularly when there is no apparent reason for it. Persistent training will soon teach the dog to speak on command with a consequent improvement in neighbour relations.
- 'Table manners' are sadly lacking in many of today's dogs. The easy solution is not to start feeding table scraps in the first place. As soon as the dog begs at the table, chastise it sharply (with your voice) and take it back to its bed.
- A dog that constantly jumps up at its owner should be made to sit while it receives a 'verbal warning'. The tone of your voice and your body language should get the message across.
- An adult dog that chews shoes, clothes or even furniture and carpets is probably bored. Make sure that it is getting enough exercise and, if you have to leave it alone for any length of time, provide a supply of chewable toys. Anything, such as slippers, that can be put away, should be.
- Sitting on comfortable armchairs and beds is not necessary to a dog, although it probably thinks so and some owners do not mind. If your dog persistently snuggles in the cosiest place, however many times you say 'no', try placing an upturned dining chair on the sofa to prevent it climbing up there the minute you go out of the room.
- Prevention is always better than cure, so try to avoid situations that might encourage a dog to behave badly.
- Consistency is essential. It is no good allowing it liberty to behave in a particular way one day and then telling it off for exactly the same thing the next.
- Finally, let us not forget that owners have bad habits, too. Allowing your dog to foul in a public place and then not poop-scooping must be one of the worst.

Body language

Observing your dog's body language gives valuable clues to how it is feeling and what course of action it is likely to take next.
- Aggression shows in a tall stance with the tail erect. The dog is trying to make itself look as big as possible. If the hackles, the bristling hairs along the neck and back, rise, the lips curl and the dog starts to snarl, it is going to attack.
- Fear shows in a low, cringing posture, with the ears flat against the head and the tail tucked under the body.
- Submission is indicated by rolling on the back to expose the vulnerable abdomen. Usually one hind leg is slightly raised. This posture is often seen in puppies, who use it to tell adult, canine strangers that they are only babies!

Cars play such a major role in modern life, it is a good idea to get your dog used to travelling from an early age.

Dogs in Cars

Cars play a large part in the way we live today. If your dog is to accompany you whenever necessary, you must make sure that it looks upon a car journey as something to be enjoyed.

Start while your puppy is young. Allowing it to become familiar with the car while it is stationary and putting the dog's own blanket or favourite toy in the car can help overcome any nervousness. Once the puppy accepts being in the car, make a short journey every day so that it gets used to the motion. It can be helpful to take a passenger who, by talking to or holding the dog, can help instil confidence. As with any kind of training, repetition is the key and in no time at all you should be able to take the dog with you wherever you travel.

There are several cautions to take note of when driving with your dog.

- Never force the dog. It will learn in its own good time to accept the car.
- The dog should always have a designated part of the car – never on the front seat. The rear compartment of a hatch-back or estate car is ideal, as the dog can be prevented from leaping to the front and possibly causing an accident. The best methods of restraint are a dog cage, a dog guard or a harness.
- Take the dog for a walk before starting a journey.
- Do not allow a dog to sit with its head out of the window. This can be very dangerous and can lead to all sorts of problems, especially with the dog's eyes.

- Do not give food or water immediately before a journey to reduce the chances of travel sickness.
- Take a bottle of water and the dog's water bowl if you are going on a long journey.
- Do not leave your dog in a parked car even when the sun is only moderate. Even with a window open, the temperature inside the car can quickly rise to an intolerable level and it is unlikely that the dog will survive.
- On a long journey, do not forget that just as you need to stop now and again, so your dog will need to stretch its legs.
- Finally, make sure that when you open the car door, *you* get out first and not the dog.

Always remember that a secure dog is a safe dog.

Public transport

- If possible, avoid travelling at the busiest times when buses and trains are very crowded.
- Always keep your dog on the lead and fully under control. Unfamiliar sounds may be frightening.
- Do not let it climb onto seats.

It is important to prevent your dog becoming overheated during a car journey. A grille fitted in the window frame allows a good flow of air, but stops the dog sticking out its head.

6

A GALLERY OF BREEDS

It is very easy for the newcomer to the world of dogs to become totally confused about which direction to go. This is understandable when you consider that there are more than 150 recognized breeds, comprising every imaginable size, coat type and colour.

●

The smaller breeds make excellent companions and are ideally suited to the not-so-active owner or to those with limited space. Medium-sized breeds are the most popular and are, therefore, the easiest to find. The large or giant breeds look impressive, but do need plenty of living space and will consume a sizeable amount of food every day.

●

This chapter provides information on more than 50 of the more popular breeds, including size, feeding, exercise and grooming requirements, as well as a guide to suitability. Obviously, not every dog you see will conform exactly to these specifications. Each dog is different but we are sure you will find these guidelines useful. Finally, do not forget that there is only one thing better than owning a dog and that is to own two or three of them.

TOY GROUP

- Bichon Frisé
- Cavalier King
  Charles Spaniel
- Chihuahua
- King Charles Spaniel
- Papillon
- Pekingese
- Pomeranian
- Pug
- Yorkshire Terrier

Bichon Frisé

This is a most adorable dog with a happy and playful disposition. It enjoys a lively romp in the country, but take heed as you may spend as much time bathing your Bichon Frisé afterwards as you did exercising it. Nevertheless, regular exercise is definitely required.

An ancient French breed, the Bichon Frisé is a very intelligent dog with an extremely dignified air. It is suited to both town and country living. Daily grooming is essential to keep its silky textured coat looking good. The coat should fall into corkscrew curls with a good, thick undercoat. The head resembles a powder puff with dark eyes.

TOY GROUP

Cavalier King Charles Spaniel

This breed lives up to its name, being 'royal' in character and possessing great presence and charm. It weighs 5–8 kg/12–18 lb and is suited to both town and country living. A lively, bright affectionate breed, it enjoys lots of exercise and makes an ideal family companion. Daily grooming of the long silky coat is essential. Colours are Black and Tan, Blenheim (pearly white with red markings), Tri-colour (black and white with tan markings) and Ruby (a rich red). A fearless character for one so small, the Cavalier King Charles Spaniel is a joy to own and returns at least twice as much affection as it is given.

Chihuahua

A loyal, affectionate and intelligent breed, the Chihuahua has the heart of a lion. It luxuriates in its owner's attention, but can be a little shy with strangers. It is not suited to outdoor living and must be kept somewhere warm and draught-free. It is an ideal breed for the elderly town-dweller and for those with limited living space. Only moderate exercise is needed. There are two different types of coat: a long and a smooth coat. Both require a minimal amount of grooming. However, the nails grow very quickly, so a regular check is necessary and you may need to clip them. Inexpensive to keep, the Chihuahua is a very long-lived dog and it is not unusual for it to reach well into its teens. When fully grown it should not weigh more than 2–3 kg/4–6 lb.

TOY GROUP

TOY GROUP

King Charles Spaniel

Despite its size, the King Charles Spaniel is a very hardy little dog. It makes an ideal family companion, loves children and enjoys being involved in every aspect of family life. It is very quick to learn and gets on well with other pets. It is not suited to living outside, but loves exercise. It is adaptable to town or country living. Daily grooming is required and the dog must be rubbed down with a towel after being out in the rain. The ears and feet are heavily feathered and should not be trimmed. The eyes need to be washed with a weak saline solution and the ears should be checked regularly for canker. The King Charles Spaniel weighs 3.5–6.5 kg/8–14 lb. The colours are Black and Tan (rich black with tan marking), Tri-colour (pearly white with black patches and tan markings on the cheeks, inner ears and over the eyes), Blenheim (pearly white with chestnut red patches) and Ruby (rich chestnut whole-coloured).

Papillon

The Papillon (left) is often called the 'butterfly dog' because of the way its ears are set. This dainty toy dog is extremely strong and remarkably healthy. It will walk most owners off their feet and you will tire long before your Papillon does. However, it will also settle for a walk in the park. Intensely loyal to its owner, it tends to resent strangers and is inclined to bark when visitors arrive. It is a very alert, intelligent dog with a lively expression. Colours are white with patches of any colour except liver. Daily grooming is required to keep the coat and fringes in good condition.

Pekingese

Despite appearing to be small and delicate, this is a very bold and independent dog. It loves to be the centre of attention and is an expert at it. Although good with children, it really prefers to be the faithful companion of an adult. The Pekingese enjoys a walk, but it is not the best breed for someone who likes to tramp miles. Take heed: if you neglect your Pekingese, you will find that it will become destructive. The coat needs daily grooming, but it is not difficult to care for. The eyes need to be washed with an eye lotion and the wrinkles should be wiped daily.

TOY GROUP

Pomeranian

This happy and amusing character is totally devoted to its owner. It is adaptable and as well-suited to living in a city apartment as a country mansion. It can become a noisy dog if left unchecked. However, the breed is eager to learn, so it is best not to let the barking become a habit. It loves to give the impression to other dogs that it is a big dog and will do this by standing on tiptoes. It is very happy as a lapdog, but also enjoys a walk. It adores being pampered and loves being groomed. Use a stiff bristle brush as it has a short, fluffy undercoat and a long topcoat. Seek expert advice on regular trimming.

Pug

The clearly-defined wrinkles are a very important feature of the head and expression in this dignified breed. The tail is curled tightly and carried over the hip. A highly intelligent dog with an extrovert character, it adapts readily to any domestic situation. It is very affectionate and good with children. It tends to be rather a greedy dog, so you must adhere to a strict diet, preventing it from indulging in its most favourite pastime of eating.

An energetic, playful breed, the Pug enjoys all forms of exercise. A minimal amount of grooming will keep the coat in the desired glossy condition.

Yorkshire Terrier

One of the most popular breeds today, the Yorkshire Terrier is affectionate, very hardy and protective to its owners. It thinks it is a much bigger dog, so it is not afraid to make friends with other animals, whatever their size. It is comfortable living in the town or the country; it is happy to play in the garden, but if you decide on a long country walk, it will certainly be able to keep up with you. In fact, you may tire long before your dog. The long silky coat is apt to look shaggy if left unattended, so regular, daily brushing is required. This also helps to remove any loose hair. You can have the coat trimmed, which will reduce the time spent on grooming. A regular bath is also required, so this is not a breed for someone who does not have the time to spend on this kind of routine care. The ideal size for an adult Yorkshire Terrier is up to 3.5 kg/7 lb.

Bulldog

Originally bred for bull-baiting, the Bulldog is very courageous and intelligent. Despite its bellicose appearance, it is very docile and enjoys joining in children's games. Nevertheless, it makes a good guard dog and is very protective towards its family. As it requires little exercise, the Bulldog is not the breed for serious walkers. It is not suited to hot weather. Take care when exercising, especially in the summer, when an early morning or late afternoon walk is probably best. The breed has a reputation for snoring, sometimes even louder than it owners. The Bulldog can be obstinate, so teach it from day one what you require of it and you will reap the benefits in later years. Do not forget, it really wants to please you, so with encouragement, it will do its utmost to reward you. Grooming is easy; a daily brushing with a stiff brush is normally all that is required. The ears, eyes and wrinkles should be inspected daily and cleaned if necessary.

UTILITY GROUP

- Bulldog
- Boston Terrier
- Chow Chow
- Dalmatian
- Japanese Akita
- Lhasa Apso
- Poodle
- Shih Tzu
- Schnauzer

Boston Terrier

The Boston Terrier is an ideal companion for the novice dog owner, as it is very affectionate, extremely obedient and adores children. A family embarking on having a dog for the first time could not start with anything easier. It loves to play and likes to have plenty of its own toys. If these are not readily available, you may find that some of the children's toys end up in the dog's bed. This is not a dog to keep in an outside kennel. Among the advantages of the Boston Terrier is that it lacks that 'doggy' smell and it sheds very little coat. Grooming is minimal – just a daily brush. Daily exercise on a lead is sufficient.

Chow Chow

The Chow Chow has a dignified and aloof expression. Originally bred to hunt, it makes an incredibly loyal companion and will defend you to the last if need be. However, this characteristic does mean that it is best exercised on the lead, as it will fight if provoked by other dogs.

While it is not a breed to walk to heel readily, with gentle persuasion it will comply with your wishes. It is a very clean animal, free from all objectionable 'doggy' smells. An unusual feature is the black tongue, a characteristic shared by some small bears. In spite of its profuse coat, a mere five-minute brush every day, with a little more attention once a week, is enough to keep it in gleaming condition. It is advisable to invest in good-quality grooming equipment.

Dalmatian

Bred to run with a horse and carriage, the Dalmatian has plenty of energy. It adores children and is happy to join in their games. Totally loyal, it loves to please its owners. When you see a litter, remember that the puppies are born white; their markings appear and become more definite as they grow. A Dalmatian will take as much exercise as you can give and this must be on a regular basis. As it is a very sociable dog and rarely fights, it is safe to let it have free-running exercise. Grooming is easy, as it is good at keeping itself clean and needs bathing only occasionally. However, Dalmatians do shed a lot of coat, but regular brushing will keep this under control.

UTILITY GROUP

Japanese Akita

The Japanese Akita was bred to hunt deer, wild boar and occasionally black bear in its native country. Over the last few years, it has gained much popularity outside Japan. It exudes great presence and strength and will act as guard dog to both your home and family. It is very intelligent, has a sound temperament and is easily trained.

Considering its size, it requires only a medium level of exercise. It loves to swim and, as it has webbed feet, it is very adept at this. Daily grooming is required, as this breed has a double coat: a medium to soft topcoat and a thick and furry undercoat.

Lhasa Apso

The word 'apso' means goat-like and this dog, which originates from Tibet, may have been used as a guard for herds of goats. Naturally suspicious of strangers, it is a very confident and affectionate breed, making an excellent companion. It is suited to both town and country living. The Lhasa Apso (above) is very lively and enjoys the company of children. It needs plenty of exercise both on and off the lead. This is a very heavily coated dog, so take heed. Grooming is not just a five-minute job; it will take you at least 20–30 minutes every day.

Poodle

There are three sizes of Poodle: miniature, toy and standard. If you have decided on this breed, all you now have to do is to match the size to your lifestyle. All Poodles have a great sense of fun and are very intelligent, with the toy and standard varieties accepting obedience training quite readily. The Poodle prefers the company of adults to being with children. Lots of exercise and play is essential; a long walk is just as acceptable as a good game in the garden. It needs regular grooming with a wire pin brush and comb and requires clipping every six weeks. This tedious task is best left to the professionals.

UTILITY GROUP

Shih Tzu

This most attractive, intelligent and loyal dog simply adores human companionship and will not take kindly to being ignored. It is not a breed to consider if you are unable to spend much time with it. It also requires a lot of time spent on grooming, by no means a small task. Daily grooming is essential, as the coat is apt to tangle if it is not properly cared for and then the task becomes very painful for the dog. The top knot is best tied up in a band to keep the hair from getting into the eyes. It is suited to town or country living, but needs regular exercise both on and off the lead.

Schnauzer

Like the Poodle, the Schnauzer comes in three sizes: miniature, standard and giant. All three varieties are excellent with children and devoted to their owners. It is a very intelligent breed with a good sense of humour. Tough and hardy, but suspicious of strangers, it makes a good guard dog. The miniature Schnauzer adapts to both town and country life, but the two larger varieties need more space and exercise. The Giant is slower to mature than the other two. The coat needs daily grooming with special attention to those wonderful whiskers. The coat also needs stripping. The breeder from whom you obtain your puppy will be able to give you instructions, or stripping can be done professionally.

UTILITY GROUP

GUNDOG GROUP

- English Setter
- Irish Setter
- German Wirehaired Pointer
- Golden Retriever
- Cocker Spaniel
- Pointer
- Labrador
- Weimaraner

English Setter

Thought to be one of the oldest of the Gundog breeds, the English Setter is a very glamourous dog. An affectionate breed, it loves to be with children, adores human company and that of other animals. It does not take kindly to being left alone for long periods, so make sure that you have time to spend with this lovely breed. As it is slow to mature, training may take some time, but there is a brain and your perseverance will be rewarded. Lots of free-ranging exercise is required. There is a variety of colours: Blue Belton (black and white), Orange or Lemon Belton (orange or lemon and white), Blue Belton and Tan (black and white and tan) and Liver Belton (liver and white). The coat needs regular daily brushing. Occasional bathing may also be required as the English Setter always seems to find dirty water in which to play. A delightful breed to own, it will repay all the love you give.

Irish Setter

The Irish Setter, also known as the Red Setter, stands taller and has a racier appearance than the English Setter. Its long, silky coat is a rich chestnut colour. The eyes are dark with a melting expression. Choosing a puppy can be difficult, as they are often as similar as peas in a pod; it is made even more difficult by the fact that litters tend to be large. The Irish Setter is an ideal family companion with a wonderful disposition. It is totally reliable with children and strangers. However, it thinks that everyone is its friend, so it is not the breed if you are looking for a guard dog. A high-spirited breed, it needs plenty of exercise, including free-running. It is a joy to watch when it is in full stride, moving with style and grace. It gets on well with other dogs, showing no signs of aggression. Daily grooming keeps the coat in gleaming condition.

GUNDOG GROUP

German Wirehaired Pointer

The German Wirehaired Pointer (left) has only relatively recently become popular outside its native country, but has quickly established a reputation as a high-quality, versatile gundog and a loyal and devoted companion. It loves water and swims very well. It is not a breed for the faint-hearted, as it requires a very firm hand. Aloof to strangers, it will protect its home and family. It accepts training willingly and is very eager to please. This breed needs a lot of exercise, otherwise it can become bored and unresponsive. The coat requires little attention and should, as the name implies, be of a wiry texture.

Golden Retriever

This very popular breed is recognized as an adaptable gundog, as well as being a first-class family companion. Widely used as a guide dog for the blind, it is very easy to train and totally trustworthy with both adults and children. The Golden Retriever (right) will always greet you on your return home with a present – probably one of your slippers, a glove or a cushion. It needs at least one hour's exercise daily, both on and off the lead. Regular brushing is required to remove any dead hair and this will help when it sheds its coat.

Cocker Spaniel

One of the smaller of the gundogs, growing only to about 37 cm/16 inches in height, the Cocker Spaniel has a reputation for giving unlimited affection to its owners and friends. Willing to please, whether working or playing games with the family, its exuberant character makes it a fun dog to live with. It requires plenty of exercise and will never tire of being taken for walks. Grooming must not be neglected, as the ears have a wealth of soft, silky feathering which must be brushed daily. Ears and eyes must be checked regularly. Traditionally the tail has always been docked, but with many veterinarians now being against this practice, you may find that your Cocker has a full tail.

Pointer

The Pointer is an extremely striking and aristocratic-looking dog. It is very adaptable and if you are looking for a working gundog and a trustworthy companion, this breed is certainly worth considering. It is willing to please and good with children and other animals. Colours are liver and white, black and white and lemon and white. There is also a solid black and a tri-colour, but these are rarely seen. The short coat is very easy to care for with just a daily brushing. In common with other Gundogs, plenty of free-running exercise is required to maintain peak condition.

Labrador

A hardy and reliable dog, the Labrador (left) is always willing to please, devoted to its owner and loves children. There is no sign of aggression or shyness in this breed, which has made it very popular as a guide dog for the blind. Being a wonderful companion with a strong retrieving instinct it is a useful and powerful working gundog, requiring lots of exercise both on and off the lead. The Labrador comes in self-colours, either black, yellow or liver-chocolate. The coat is short and dense with a hard feel to the touch. Grooming is minimal: only a thorough daily brushing.

GUNDOG GROUP

Weimaraner

The Weimaraner (right) is a hunting dog and is at its best when it is given a job to do. Fearless, friendly and protective of its family and home, it is a very intelligent breed, capable of being trained to a high standard of obedience. Nevertheless it requires a firm hand. The most striking feature of the Weimaraner is its colour: silver-grey on the body and slightly lighter on the head and ears. The coat has the appearance of a metallic sheen. The eyes are amber to blue-grey. It is a very adaptable breed, needing lots of exercise, but requires little grooming as the dirt simply drops out of the coat.

Bearded Collie

A very attractive looking dog, the Bearded Collie is lively, confident and makes a very good family companion. It is intelligent and easy to train. It enjoys family life and is reliable with children, joining in their games and activities.

As it has boundless energy, it needs lots of exercise both on and off the lead. Colours are any shade of grey, from silver to almost black, and shades of brown, from fawn to reddish brown. It has a double coat: the undercoat is soft and close and the topcoat is harsh, strong and flat. Plenty of grooming is required to keep the long flowing coat in tiptop condition. An occasional bath is usually also necessary.

Bernese

The Bernese (below) originates from Switzerland where it is used for herding and as a draught dog. A most beautiful and impressive breed, it grows to 67 cm/ 27 inches, so requires plenty of living space. It is an affectionate companion, valued as a house guard and easily trained. It also gets on well with other animals. The colour is jet black with tan markings on the legs and over the eyes, with white symmetrical head markings and white chest, paws and tip of tail. The coat is long and silky and requires regular grooming. Medium exercise will keep this gentle giant in good condition.

WORKING GROUP

Border Collie

The Border Collie (above) has an unrivalled reputation for working with cattle and sheep and is a consistent winner in obedience competitions. It is loyal, intelligent and makes a good family companion. As it is essentially a working dog, it is not really suited to town life, preferring the wide open spaces of the countryside. It is as happy walking to heel as working on the farm, but with its stamina and brains it is at its best when given a job to do. Its natural herding instincts will always come out; if there are no animals to herd, it will happily herd people together.

Rottweiler

Originating from the town of Rottweil, Germany, where it is known as the *Rottweiler Metzgerhund* or Rottweil Butcher's Dog, this powerful breed requires firm but kind handling. It makes a wonderful companion, is highly intelligent and totally devoted to its family. Consequently, it makes a superb guard dog. A puppy must not be over-exercised and must have a good-quality diet, as it needs to do a lot of growing in a very short space of time. Socialization is very important from as early as possible. Local puppy training classes are an excellent idea. When fully grown, a Rottweiler may weigh in excess of 56 kg/125 lb and has the appearance of an animal with great confidence and immense strength. Regular exercise on and off the lead helps to maintain this breed in peak condition. The coat is very easy to care for, requiring only a good daily brushing.

Rough Collie

The Rough Collie is famed in Scotland as the guardian of large flocks of sheep and is popular in both Britain and the United States. Queen Victoria bred collies and took a special interest in improving the breed. It is an ideal family companion as it is affectionate and loyal. Of medium size with a gentle disposition, it is easily trained and adapts to any size of house. It is a very hardy breed. It is good with children, but a little apprehensive of strangers; it will decide for itself and in its own time if newcomers are acceptable. It requires regular exercise both on and off the lead. Do not let the profuse and magnificent coat put you off because the grooming is, in fact, relatively easy; just daily grooming is all that is required.

Great Dane

Used in the seventeenth century for hunting wild boar, the Great Dane (right) has evolved into an adaptable breed that will not object to living in a cottage or a castle, as long as it has plenty of exercise. A sociable dog, devoted to its family, it also gets along well with other animals. It is elegant and graceful, with an air of dash and daring. Never play rough-and-tumble with a Great Dane puppy because it will not be easy to stop this game once it is fully grown. It measures over 75 cm/ 30 inches to the shoulder and weighs 54 kg/120 lb. The coat is easy to look after and just requires daily brushing.

Pembroke Welsh Corgi

Originally bred in South Wales by farmers and used for herding and driving cattle and ponies, the Pembroke Welsh Corgi (left) has been popular with the British Royal Family for many years, with the result that it is one of the best-known breeds in Britain. It is a devoted companion, a hardy and intelligent dog who will tolerate children. It is easily trained but can become disobedient in the hands of a weak owner. Regular exercise is most important – remember its working background. The coat is water-resistant so sheds dirt itself. Just a daily brushing is required.

Samoyed

Originally used as a herding and guarding dog, this is a very striking member of the Spitz family, devoted to its owner and thriving on human company. It can be slightly independent and requires firm but kind handling. It loves the wide open countryside, but will happily live as a town dog if given plenty of regular exercise. The coat requires brushing and combing for about 10–15 minutes several times a week. Care must be taken if the coat gets wet: it should be towelled down. Once a year, the Samoyed sheds its soft undercoat and it is best to bath your dog at this time. Comb out as much of the undercoat as possible while it is wet. Dry the coat and comb it through again. This will remove most of the undercoat and save time spent removing it from your carpets.

Dobermann

The Dobermann (or Dobermann Pinscher) originated in Germany in the 1860s and 1870s and is now very popular all over the world. It is agile, fast and very skilled at tracking, so it is often used by the police and security services. Being intelligent and loyal, it will protect its home and family if necessary. It is extremely aloof towards people outside the family and sometimes requires the reassurance of a family member before accepting the presence of a stranger.

It does not like the cold, so if it is to live outside, its kennel must be draught-proof and warm. Its favourite place is next to the fire, or failing that, beside a radiator.

Most Dobermanns are black and tan, but there are also brown and tan and blue and tan varieties. It requires a minimum of 40 minutes daily exercise, preferably off the lead. The short coat is very easy to care for, requiring only a rub down with a Turkish towel or chamois leather to remove loose hair.

Bull Mastiff

The Bull Mastiff developed from crossing the Mastiff with the Bulldog. It was used on large country estates as a guard against poachers. It had a reputation for ferocity, but much has been done to stabilize the breed and there is now no inherent vice. In fact, it is quite a 'big softy' and despite its size, will often try to sit on your lap! It is not a breed to be taken lightly; a very large and powerful animal, it can weigh anything up to 59 kg/130 lb. It is playful and if you encourage it to be boisterous, you will find it very difficult to remain upright. Training should start at a very early age as this breed grows at an alarming rate. When fully grown, it will eat up to 1 kg/ 2 lb of meat a day. Regular exercise is required, but this should not be done by a child who would find it impossible to hold onto the lead. Regular brushing keeps the coat in good condition.

Airedale Terrier

The Airedale Terrier originated in Yorkshire and is the largest member of this group. Once used for otter hunting, it has now become a very popular companion. It has a very sporty appearance and makes a faithful and loyal pet who will guard its family and home. It will adapt to living in a confined space, but must be given exercise at least twice a day. It is happy with a walk in the park, but really enjoys the open countryside. It can live inside or outside, but any kennel must be draught-proof. The coat is hard to the touch with a soft undercoat. Daily grooming with a stiff brush is required and the coat needs to be stripped out by hand in the spring and summer. The breeder from whom you obtain your puppy will you show you how to do this. If you are unable to master the art, then do not worry as it can be done at your local dog-grooming parlour. Stripping the coat is important, otherwise you will end up with something that looks like a woolly bear.

Border Terrier

From the border counties of England and Scotland, this Terrier (right) was bred to hunt the fox. It is a good companion: loyal, affectionate and likes children. Be very careful when training a Border Terrier, as it dislikes rough treatment and sometimes even a cross word will hurt it. It wants to please, so it can be taught very easily. It requires plenty of exercise and it is unfair to keep this dog if you cannot devote sufficient time to this. It is not unknown for a Border Terrier to go off hunting on its own, sometimes for several days at a time. The coat requires stripping twice a year.

Cairn Terrier

This breed (left) from the Highlands of Scotland is now very popular all over the world. This is not surprising as it makes a wonderful family companion who enjoys being with children. It is intelligent with a bright and lively disposition. It loves attention, but does not get upset if it is left at home when the family goes out for the day. It can live indoors or out and is very hardy. It requires moderate exercise, but is just as content playing with the children in the park as running across open fields. The coat is hard enough to be water-resistant and should always look rugged.

Bedlington Terrier

The origins of this breed are somewhat uncertain, but it is thought that the Greyhound or Whippet played some part and, possibly, also the Otterhound. The Bedlington Terrier is very striking in its lamb-like appearance. This is deceptive because it is full of courage and capable of 'looking after' itself. It is an ideal family companion, who adores children, is quick to learn and is gaining much success in obedience competitions. It adapts to town or country living, as long as adequate walks are given – remember it is a lively breed. This is the ideal dog for the house-proud as it does not shed its coat. Even the dead hairs stay in the coat until combed out. Daily brushing will keep it in good condition. The coat does require regular trimming, otherwise it will become tangled.

Dandie Dinmont Terrier

The Dandie Dinmont (right) was used to hunt badgers, otters and foxes. It is now mostly seen as a companion who is totally devoted to its owner. It can be aloof with strangers. The breed has a strong character, is intelligent and possesses a good sense of humour. It is not suited to living outside in a kennel and is not good if kept with a large number of other dogs. It is a good house dog with a bark that will deter most intruders. It is very adaptable when it comes to exercise; it is happy out walking or sitting on your lap all day. It needs daily grooming with a brush and comb.

Staffordshire Bull Terrier

Derived from crossing the Bulldog with one or more of the Terrier breeds, the Staffordshire (left) was used for bull- and bear-baiting and later for badger- and dog-fighting. Now, the 'Staffie' is a valued companion. Beneath its somewhat fearsome exterior, it is very gentle and good with children, but still makes an excellent guard dog. It needs firm handling from the early stages. It requires only moderate exercise but do not let it off the lead if there are other dogs around, as it will not be able to resist a fight. The coat requires little attention: a quick daily brushing.

TERRIER GROUP

West Highland White Terrier

The West Highland White Terrier originates from Scotland. A small, game, hardy Terrier, it was originally used to hunt fox and badger. It is now a very popular family companion, good with children and other dogs. It adapts to town or country life, but loves the wide open countryside best. It is intelligent, so it is easy to train. When it comes to exercise, it is as happy walking on the lead as it is free-running in the country, or will settle for a game with a ball. Afterwards, it loves nothing better than to curl up by the fireside. The coat is 'pure' white and needs daily brushing. It also needs stripping twice a year to remove any surplus hair. You can do it yourself or take it to the local dog-grooming parlour.

Parson Jack Russell

The Parson Jack Russell originated in Devon and was the result of years of breeding by the Rev. John Russell – hence the name. It was bred to go underground and bolt the fox and is now a very popular working dog, as well as being a valued companion. An affectionate, sporty little dog, it is in its element in the countryside, either ferreting or after foxes. Regular exercise is essential as it has boundless energy. It can become over-excited and yappy if it is not kept properly under control; do this while it is young. The coat requires only minimal daily brushing and no stripping or trimming is needed.

Afghan Hound

A hunting dog originating from Afghanistan, this is now a very popular breed. A glamourous dog, it gives the impression of strength, dignity, speed and power. It is reputed to be aloof but is very affectionate to its owners and children. Being a hound, it does have an independent streak and can be quite headstrong at times. It is therefore important to show your Afghan that you are in charge right from the start. It loves affection and has a great sense of humour. It needs plenty of living space and plenty of exercise, both on and off the lead, to use up its boundless energy. Colours vary from fawn to silver, grey, black and tan, blue and red brindle. The long flowing coat is the Afghan's glory but maintaining it requires a lot of hard work. It is not shed and as it is thick and fine, it tends to mat. Brush it layer by layer and it is best to invest in good-quality grooming equipment.

Basset Hound

The Basset Hound is used today to hunt hare. Although it makes an ideal family companion that is wonderful with children, it is still a hound and if allowed to escape from your garden, may well wander for miles. You must be sympathetic when training a Basset Hound, as it is slow to learn and not always obedient – unless it decides to be. It is fair to say that unless you have plenty of patience and time to spend on this breed, then it is not the dog for you. Naturally used to large packs, it prefers company. Minimal grooming is needed but regular inspection of the ears and nails is required.

HOUND GROUP

HOUND GROUP

Beagle

The Beagle (right) is used to hunt hare. It is very popular as a companion, as it is jolly, affectionate and intelligent. It loves children and gets on well with other pets. It is very adaptable to living in the town or the country. A healthy and sturdy dog, it loves exercise. Although it is very good at keeping itself fit, it must have regular exercise both on and off the lead. As with all hounds, you must make sure your garden is secure, as if allowed to escape, the Beagle will wander for miles. The coat is short and weatherproof so requires only the minimal amount of grooming.

Borzoi

The Borzoi comes from Russia where it was used for hunting wolf and coursing. It really is the most aristocratic of the hounds. It is calm, dignified and a wonderful companion. It said to be aloof with strangers and only show affection to those it accepts. Being a reserved and gentle dog, it is unenthusiastic about playing games with children. It requires a lot of exercise; remember that it is a hunter, so do not let it off the lead until you are far away from livestock. The elegant coat is long and silky, but surprisingly easy to care for with just the minimum of daily brushing.

Dachshund

The Dachshund originated in Germany and was bred as a badger hound. It is courageous, loyal and intelligent with a fun sense of humour. It likes children, but is wary of strangers. Despite its short legs, it will take as much exercise as you want. There are three different coat types: smooth-haired (above), longhaired and wirehaired. There are also two different sizes: miniature and standard. The miniature weighs up to 5 kg/11 lb and the standard up to 9 kg/20 lb. Colours vary from red, chocolate, brindle, dapple to black and tan. All three types of coat are very easy to care for with the minimum of grooming.

HOUND GROUP

Irish Wolfhound

Originally used in Ireland to hunt wolf, stag and boar, the Irish Wolfhound has a super temperament and is marvellous with children. It really is a gentle giant until provoked. Firm, gentle handling is required as it is apt to have a mind of its own, but is also willing to please. Despite its size – and this can be in excess of 79 cm/31 inches to the shoulder – it does not require a great deal of exercise. A walk on a lead or a gentle trot by your side will keep it happy. The colours vary from a pale cream to black. The coat has a rough, hard feel to it and requires regular brushing.

Whippet

The Whippet (right) is an ideal choice for those who want a gentle, affectionate companion. It is good with children and impeccably clean in the house. Slow to mature, it does like its home comforts and must be kept out of draughts, so it is not suited to living outside. When it comes to exercise, remember that this is a racing dog and capable of running at speeds of up to 64 kph/40 mph. It needs adequate, regular exercise, including free-running as well as walking on the lead. The coat is short and very easy to care for with the minimum of grooming required. The nails require clipping.

HOUND GROUP

Saluki

For centuries, the Saluki, together with the horse, has been the prized possession of the Arab nations, where it is still used to hunt gazelle. It makes an ideal companion as it is affectionate, intelligent and good with children. While aloof to strangers and a good guard dog, it is never aggressive. A very healthy breed, it requires a lot of exercise. As this is a hunting dog, take care when you are exercising it off the lead. Two of the many lovely things about the Saluki are that it is odour-free and requires only minimal grooming with a soft brush and a hand glove.

7

HEALTH CARE

It would be unreasonable and highly unlikely to expect your dog to be perfectly healthy for the whole of its life. It may develop some kind of illness or even have an accident at some stage and however much we try to protect our pets through immunization (see page 41) and proper care, these things do happen. This chapter covers useful first aid treatment for emergencies and provides information on some common canine ailments and how to recognize their symptoms. It is impossible to include everything and, unfortunately, you will not qualify as a veterinarian after reading this chapter. Always bear in mind that it is unwise for you to treat your dog yourself – possibly for something you do not fully understand – without first obtaining your veterinarian's opinion. Never give your dog medication designed for humans, as you could actually cause further damage.

Regular grooming (see pages 32-38) enables you to inspect the skin for parasites and skin irritation, the mouth for tartar build-up on the teeth, loose teeth and bad breath, the ears for excessive wax and any unpleasant smell, the eyes for inflammation and discharge and the feet for length of the nails and dew claws. Any problems that can be addressed at an early stage may then require only a short course of treatment, thus minimizing your veterinary bill.

As your dog grows up, you will soon learn to detect if it is really ill or just 'off colour'. Just like us, dogs have their 'off' days. Any departure from normal behaviour should be monitored carefully. Remember your veterinarian is probably only a telephone call away and it is always better to be safe than sorry.

In the later years of your dog's life, even if it appears to be in the best of health, it is advisable to have at least one annual veterinary check-up.

COMPLEMENTARY AND ALTERNATIVE THERAPIES

Complementary or alternative medicine is becoming increasingly accepted as a recognized form of treatment for animal as well as human ailments. In fact, much of modern medicine is derived directly from some forms of traditional alternative therapy. The terms 'complementary' and 'alternative' embrace any form of therapy outside the mainstream. Although modern medicine can cure some acute diseases, the drugs used sometimes have unpleasant side effects and this is enough for some people to choose alternative therapies. There are veterinarians who prefer to use complementary therapies whenever possible, especially for treating older animals, and their numbers are increasing weekly. Listed below are just a few of

It is advisable to consult your veterinarian if your dog is 'off colour' or has a minor injury.

Bach Flower Remedies

These are made from infusions of various flowers in water preserved in alcohol. Rescue Remedy, a combination of five other Remedies, was designed for treating shock and extreme stress. Intended for human treatment, Rescue Remedy can also be given to dogs to relieve the symptoms of trauma. A dispensing dropper is supplied with the bottle and one or two drops can be put directly on the dog's tongue for instant effect in an emergency. For longer-term use, add a couple of drops to the water bowl each day.

the most widely used alternative therapies. Always consult your veterinarian for a full diagnosis before seeking referral to an alternative practitioner.

Acupuncture

This is one aspect of traditional Chinese medicine whereby ultra-fine needles are inserted at specific points along the meridian lines of the body. Each acupuncture point is thought to have its own specific function in maintaining good health and a balanced 'whole'. As the needles are so extremely fine, going only a few millimetres into the skin, they do not cause pain. Acupuncture has been very effective in treating digestive problems, allergies, skin disorders and auto-immune disorder.

Homeopathy

This is the medical practice of treating like with like. In other words, an illness is treated with a substance (in a heavily diluted form) that produces the same symptoms as those apparent in the sick animal. Like traditional Chinese medicine, homeopathy addresses the whole organism, rather than simply treating only the specific ailment or disease. Consequently, a homeopathic veterinarian or practitioner will require a very detailed picture of your dog – healthy and ill – to form a complete profile before prescribing treatment. Homeopathy is a very gentle form of treatment to which animals often respond positively. It can address a broad spectrum of conditions, has no known adverse side effects and can be particularly useful with elderly dogs and those suffering from allergies.

Herbalism

This ancient method of treatment uses the flowers, bark, leaves and seeds of plants as preventatives and curatives. Dogs have always sought out specific grasses when they feel 'off colour' and herbalism could be seen as merely an extension of this. Once again, herbal practitioners tend to take a holistic approach to treatment.

Many commercial brands of tablets and tinctures are available from pet shops; it is always advisable to use a remedy designed specifically for dogs rather than one prepared for human consumption. Always follow the manufacturer's instructions, whether for a specific treatment or as a general health booster. The ability of herbal remedies to be used in a wide range of conditions has contributed to its recent increase in popularity.

Osteopathy and Chiropractic

These therapies use manipulation techniques, in slightly different ways, to detect and correct faulty structure and function of the body and spine. The words comes from Greek – osteon (bone) and pathos (suffering) and cheir (hand) and praktikos (practical). This form of treatment can be very beneficial after a joint or muscular injury and for treating rheumatism.

Dietary Control

Nowadays, the manufacturers of commercial dog foods are aware of specific dietary requirements. For example, low-fat and low-cholesterol foods are thought to reduce the chance of heart problems.

Animal Behaviourists

It is thought that some obstinate conditions and disorders may, in fact, have psychological rather than physiological causes, Consequently, they may not respond to either conventional or complementary therapies. Some veterinarians now are referring dogs to animal behaviourists, not just for treatment of anti-social problems, such as aggression (see page 64), but also for a range of other ailments, such as skin disorders.

THE ANATOMY OF THE DOG

The skeleton of the dog is made up of a series of bones held together by ligaments, tendons and muscles. The body shape and the size of individual bones vary according to the breed and size of the dog, but with only a few exceptions, all dogs have the same number of bones, Do not forget, however, that a dog with a docked tail will have fewer tail bones than individuals with full-length tails.

The skull of the dog imparts individuality to a breed and there is great variation in the individual bones. For example, a breed such as the Afghan Hound has a long narrow skull, whereas the Cavalier King Charles Spaniel has a short, broad skull, yet they both have an identical number of components.

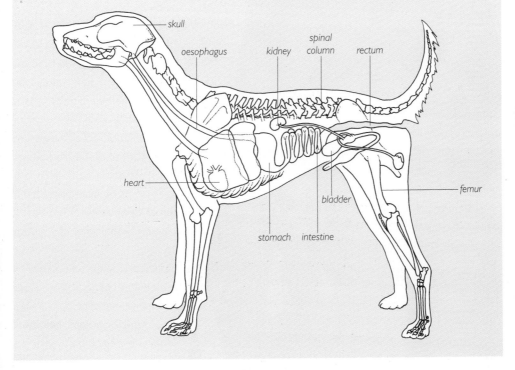

skull
oesophagus
kidney
spinal column
rectum
heart
bladder
femur
stomach   intestine

Dew claws

Not all breeds of dog have dew claws, a fifth digit and claw. Where they are present, they usually occur on the inside of the lower forelegs. Occasionally, they occur on the hindlegs. Removal is usually recommended in this case. However, two breeds, the Pyrenean Mountain Dog and the Briard or Berger de Brie, are characterized by having double hind dew claws.

Docking

Docking dogs' tails was originally introduced as a way of preventing working dogs, particularly gundogs, from severe injury caused by trapping their tails in undergrowth. It then became fashionable and the tails of many 'non-working' dogs were docked simply because it was thought to look attractive. Modern veterinarians are increasingly unwilling to perform this surgery for purely 'cosmetic' reasons, so breeds whose tails were always docked formerly are now being seen with full tails.

FIRST AID

First aid kit

- Roll of plaster
- Bandages
- Cotton wool/absorbent cotton
- Cotton buds/tips
- Blunt-ended scissors
- Tweezers
- Sterile dressing for grazes and cuts
- Antiseptic solution suitable for dogs
- Clinical thermometer

As most veterinarians are generally easily accessible these days, it is not so essential for you to be an expert in first aid as, perhaps, it once was. Nevertheless, it is advisable to keep a first aid kit for your dog and to familiarize yourself with some basic treatment that you can administer before seeking professional help.

In dogs, as with humans, the body temperature is a valuable guide to the state of health, so ask your veterinarian to show you how to use a thermometer correctly. The normal temperature of a dog is 38.6°C/101.5°F but, again like humans, this can vary slightly, so a degree or so either side is nothing to worry about. If you are unsure whether your dog is actually ill or just feeling slightly out of sorts, taking its temperature will ascertain if veterinary attention is required.

Listed below are a few common situations where you may be able to help with treatment while awaiting veterinary assistance.

Bites and Stings

Animal bites: see Fight Injuries (page 116).

Bee and wasp stings: common in the summer months, these can be extremely painful. If you can see the sting, remove it with tweezers, if possible, and, in any case, you should consult your veterinarian. Meanwhile, vinegar can ease the discomfort of wasp stings. If the sting is on or in the mouth, considerable swelling may occur which can block the airways and endanger the dog's life. Seek urgent veterinary assistance. An ice cube in the dog's mouth or an ice pack around its throat may temporarily ease the discomfort while you are getting help.

Snake bites: some countries are fortunate in having few – or even no – indigenous venomous snakes. In countries where poisonous snakes are common, if your dog has been bitten and you are

Dogs quickly learn to compensate for the temporary discomfort and awkwardness of a bandaged leg.

absolutely certain that the snake is not venomous, treat as for any other kind of bite. If you *know* the snake is venomous or you are simply *not sure*, seek urgent veterinary assistance so that an antiserum can be administered. Give the veterinarian as clear and precise a description of the snake as you can, so that he or she can administer the appropriate antiserum. Applying a tourniquet is very much a last resort; in unskilled hands, it may cause tissue death, gangrene and, ultimately, amputation.

Spider bites: some countries have indigenous, venomous spiders. Treat as for snake bite and seek immediate veterinary assistance.

Burns and Scalds

Both burns caused by direct contact with a hot surface and scalds caused by boiling liquid require immediate treatment. If possible, gently run cold water over the injured area for several minutes to reduce the pain and tissue trauma. Do not apply ointments or lotions, unless advised by your veterinarian, and never 'burst' any blisters. Get the dog to the veterinarian as soon as possible.

Chemical burns require the same treatment, but present the additional risk of injuring the dog's tongue and mouth if it licks the affected area. Moreover, depending on the chemical, licking may also result in poisoning. A muzzle, improvised with a strip of bandage, is the easiest way of preventing this. Seek immediate veterinary attention and, if there is time, rinse the affected area with plenty of clean cold water. Take the chemical container with you to the veterinarian if possible.

Choking

It is easy for a dog to get a splinter of wood or bone stuck in its mouth or throat. If you can get help, ask someone to restrain the dog and open its mouth. If possible, remove the splinter with tweezers. However, if the foreign object is firmly stuck, do not poke around as you may hurt the dog and will almost certainly cause it to panic. Seek *urgent* veterinary attention.

Cuts and Abrasions

Clean minor injuries with damp cotton wool/absorbent cotton. Trim the fur around the cut with blunt-ended scissors if necessary and apply veterinary antiseptic. Gently press a soft pad over more serious, profusely bleeding wounds to stem the bleeding and seek urgent veterinary assistance. Do not apply a tourniquet (see Snake bites, opposite).

Drowning

Most dogs enjoy swimming, but can get into trouble if caught by an underwater hazard or if they have difficulty getting out of a steep-sided water-course. If the dog is not breathing, you will need to act quickly. Pick up a small dog by its back legs and shake firmly but gently to try to clear the lungs; avoid causing whiplash injury to its neck. If this does not work, place the dog on its side and give mouth-to-mouth resuscitation as for a baby or young child. Place a large dog on its side as soon as you have lifted it out of the water, with its body raised higher than its head so the water drains from its lungs. Wait 30 seconds and then give mouth-to-mouth resuscitation as for a baby or young child.

Improvising a muzzle

An injured dog is likely to be frightened and in pain, so it may snap at anyone trying to help it. A simple but effective muzzle can be improvised with a bandage, tie, scarf or similar, soft length of fabric. Loop the bandage over the dog's muzzle and cross it over above the nose. Then loop it around the jaws, cross over the ends and tie in a secure but not tight bow behind the dog's neck (see above). This is also a useful method of preventing a dog licking any toxic substances on its paws or coat while you are obtaining veterinary assistance.

Electric Shock

Puppies, in particular, are fascinated by electrical cables and may chew through them. If the cable is live, the puppy may suffer an electric shock. *Do not touch the puppy until you have switched off the appliance/socket* or you will be electrocuted as well. Rush your dog to the veterinarian *immediately*. If professional help is not immediately available, you may need to give mouth-to-mouth resuscitation as for a baby or child. If there is no detectable pulse, apply heart massage by pushing firmly against the side of the puppy's chest just above the breast bone (see left).

Fight Injuries

If your dog has been involved in a fight, it may be difficult to see just how many wounds there are because of its fur. Examine the dog thoroughly and when you find a wound, trim the surrounding fur and bathe the wound with veterinary antiseptic solution. If the wounds look as if they require stitching, then you should seek *urgent* veterinary advice. If the injuries seem slight, keep an eye on the dog and take it to the veterinarian at a convenient time for a check-up. Puncture wounds often show little exterior damage, but may be serious. Consult your veterinarian.

Heatstroke

A dog suffering from heatstroke may foam at the mouth and even vomit. Move it immediately to a cool place. Sponge its head and face with cold water, then place cold wet towels over its body and pour over cold water as they warm up. Seek veterinary assistance.

Poisoning

To prevent your dog coming into contact with poisonous substances make sure that all human medicines are well out of reach and do not put down any rodent poison or use herbicides where the dog may come into contact with them. Even simply walking on ground that has been treated with some weedkillers can be fatal, as the dog may lick its paws afterwards.

Some modern weedkillers have no antidote, so if you think your dog has eaten poison, immediately give an emetic to make it vomit. A strong solution of salt in water will suffice. Then take it immediately to the veterinarian. If you know what has caused the poisoning and you can find the container easily, take it with you as it may help him or her select the correct treatment. Do not give an emetic if the dog has swallowed a caustic chemical.

Road Accidents

A dog injured in a road accident must be moved with the utmost care to avoid further injury. If possible, enlist the help of two or three other people and, supporting the head, back and hips, gently lift the dog onto a blanket, coat or something similar. The dog can then be moved with two people holding the corners of the blanket, keeping it taut, and the third supporting the dog's back from underneath. If you cannot find help, place the blanket along the dog's back and gently ease its body onto it, section-by-section, before gently pulling the dog to a safe place. Seek urgent veterinary help.

The dog will be suffering from shock (see opposite), so it should be kept warm with a

Warning

Dogs should never be left in a parked car. Even with a window open, the interior temperature increases very quickly to intolerable, often fatal, levels.

blanket while you are taking it to the veterinarian. Do not give the dog anything to eat or drink in case an anaesthetic will be necessary.

If there is any bleeding, apply light pressure to the bleeding point by gently pressing a pad over the area. Take care not to press too hard or you may cause further damage.

Veterinarians normally operate a 24-hour service, so do not delay in seeking help.

Shock

A dog suffering any traumatic injury is likely to be in shock. Keep it quiet and warm. Talk in kind, reassuring tones, offering the comfort of a familiar voice. Homeopathic remedies have proved useful in these circumstances and Bach's Rescue Remedy is widely recommended for both traumatized dogs and humans.

COMMON AILMENTS

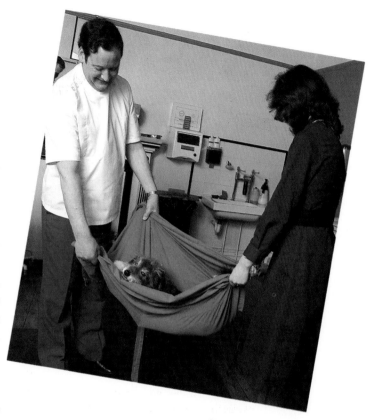

Abscess

This can appear anywhere on a body and consists of a raised, pus-filled, swollen area that is very painful. The swelling increases until eventually it bursts and discharges pus and blood. Abscess can be treated with a hot poultice and a course of antibiotics. An untreated abscess can lead to more serious complications, so always consult your veterinarian.

Anal Problems

Two small scent glands on either side of the rectum are present in both dogs and bitches. These anal glands normally empty during bowel movement, but if this fails to happen, the dog will suffer discomfort. Signs to look for are the dog dragging its bottom along the ground or continually biting under its tail. The anal glands can be expressed very easily by a veterinarian and it is possible to learn how to do this yourself.

Arthritis and Rheumatism

These conditions are seen more often in the older dog and manifest themselves in stiffness of the joints. It is important, if your dog has either condition, to keep it warm and dry and you must not allow it to become overweight, as this puts extra stress on swollen and stiff joints. Treatment with modern drugs or complementary medicine can give some relief from the pain.

An injured dog is best lifted by means of a large sheet or blanket with two people holding the corners.

Ear drops

Never put drops in your dog's ear, except on veterinary advice.
• Lift the ear flap, if necessary, and gently clean away any visible dirt or wax with damp cotton wool/absorbent cotton. Do not poke inside the ear.
• Hold the dog's head still, tilted slightly to one side, to give you clear access to the ear.
• Place the nozzle of the bottle just inside the ear; do not poke it deeply into the ear.
• Administer the required number of drops.
• Still holding the dog's head, drop the ear flap and massage very gently to encourage the drops to penetrate.
• Clean off any dribbles with cotton wool/absorbent cotton.

Bad Breath

This condition worries many dog owners. It is frequently caused by bad teeth, tartar, gum infection or incorrect diet and the dog should have a visit to the veterinarian to establish which of these is the culprit. If the teeth are decayed, they will need to be removed. A tartar build-up must also be removed. Prevention is better than cure, so always keep your dog's teeth clean and check them regularly (see page 38).

Cystitis

This is an inflammation of the bladder causing the dog to urinate frequently or to dribble urine. It is sometimes accompanied by vomiting. You may also see blood in the urine. If the cystitis is caused by a stone, the dog may be unable to urinate. In any case, it is advisable to consult your veterinarian.

Diabetes

The first signs of diabetes are severe thirst and considerable loss of weight. If diabetes is diagnosed in the early stages and it is a mild case, it may be possible to control it simply by diet. More severely affected dogs may have to take oral medicine and some will need insulin injections on a daily basis.

Diarrhoea

This can occur for many reasons; even stress or a simple over-indulgence in food can bring on an attack. Give no food for 24 hours, but provide frequent, small quantities of cooled, boiled water or ice cubes. If the diarrhoea stops within the 24-hour period, feeding can recommence with a very light diet of white meat and rice. If it continues, you must consult your veterinarian. If the dog has other signs of illness, such as blood in the faeces, vomiting or marked lethargy, do not delay for 24 hours, but consult your veterinarian immediately.

Ear Infections

Dogs with ear flaps that hang down are particularly prone to ear infections because of the lack of air to the ear. The warm, moist ear is, therefore, an ideal breeding place for fungi and bacteria. If you notice your dog shaking its head, holding its head on one side or scratching at the ear flap, it is likely to have an ear infection. On inspection, you may find a dark brown discharge or the ear flap may feel warm or swollen to the touch. If the case is mild, it may be treatable with ear drops prescribed by your veterinarian. In severe cases, the dog may have to have an anaesthetic so that its ears can be thoroughly cleaned out. Prevention is better than cure, so check ears regularly (see page 38) to prevent the worst occurring.

Eclampsia

This is an extremely serious condition seen in recently whelped bitches. If left unattended, it can be fatal, so immediate veterinary attention is vital. The bitch may be unable to walk, will be distressed and may even have convulsions. Caused by a lack of calcium in the blood, eclampsia is easily treated with an injection of calcium. The response is almost immediate. The vital importance of urgent treatment cannot be over-emphasized.

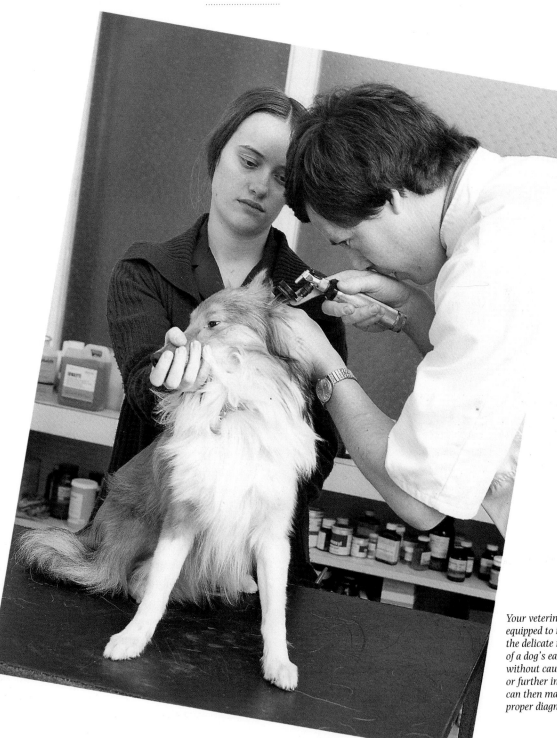

Your veterinarian is equipped to inspect the delicate interior of a dog's ears without causing pain or further injury and can then make a proper diagnosis.

Giving medicine

If you are left-handed, reverse the position of your hands in the following instructions.
• Have one of your dog's favourite treats ready to hand.
• Place your left hand over your dog's muzzle and raise its head slightly.
• Gently press the jaws with the thumb and index finger of your left hand to open the dog's mouth.
• When the dog opens its mouth, slide your left thumb into the space behind the right canine and press gently on the roof of the mouth to keep it open.
• Pop the tablet on the base of the dog's tongue with your right hand.
• Close the dog's mouth and gently hold it shut with your left hand, while massaging the throat with your right hand to encourage it to swallow.
• When you are sure that the tablet has been swallowed, release the dog and give it the treat as a reward.
• If the dog refuses to swallow, keep holding its mouth closed and place the treat near its nose. Its mouth will water and the dog will swallow.

Eczema

This skin condition is common in dogs, especially in hot weather. It can be caused by a great number of things, including diet, sensitivity to a particular item in its surroundings, stress, parasites or it can even be hereditary. A change of diet to white meat and rice can be beneficial, but this must be maintained for at least two weeks in order to quantify any improvement. If this has no effect, your veterinarian may want to take a skin scraping to establish the cause.

Haematoma

This is a large blood blister under the skin. It can occur anywhere on the body, but is most common on the ear flap (see below) and is usually caused by a knock or by continual shaking and scratching of the ear as seen with an ear infection (see page 118). If the haematoma is small, it may disperse on its own, but larger ones may require surgery. Consult your veterinarian.

Hip Dysplasia

The main symptom of hip dysplasia is lameness in the hindquarters caused by the failure of the head of the femur (thigh bone) to fit into the pelvic socket (hip). You may notice that after a walk, your dog has a problem in getting up out of its bed or even cries in pain. Your veterinarian is likely to suggest an X-ray to see if hip dysplasia is present and, if so, to what degree. It can vary from being so mild as to be almost unnoticeable to severe enough to warrant hip replacement surgery. It can be very painful. Responsible breeders of breeds with a predisposition to this problem now have the dam and sire X-rayed for hip dysplasia before breeding from them.

Vomiting

A dog can vomit at will, but a bout of continued vomiting is probably a sign that it has eaten something that does not agree with it. Initially, 24-hour starvation is recommended, with only small drinks of water or even an ice cube for it to crunch. If you give lots of water, the dog will drink it and the whole process of vomiting will start again, resulting in dehydration. If after 24 hours, the vomiting has stopped completely and the dog is looking brighter, resume normal feeding with a light diet. It is advisable to divide the dog's meal into two, especially for those that tend to eat very quickly. Should the vomiting continue, you must seek veterinary advice as it could be indicative of a more serious complaint. Equally, if there is blood in the vomit or the dog shows other signs of illness, such as diarrhoea or severe lethargy, do not delay 24 hours but consult your veterinarian immediately.

Pyometra

This is a common condition caused by an accumulation of pus or by an infection in the uterus. It is normally seen about nine weeks after a bitch has been in season. Symptoms are increased consumption of water, listlessness, raised temperature and a swollen abdomen. Take the bitch to the veterinarian immediately, as this is a very serious condition. If left untreated, pyometra can prove to be fatal.

Travel Sickness

Some dogs respond well to a drink of 1 teaspoon of glucose powder dissolved in 2 tablespoons of water just before setting out on a journey. Some alternative therapies have proved useful in dealing with car sickness. There are many different brands of travel sickness pills suitable for dogs on the market if all else fails; ask your veterinarian. It is worth getting your dog used to travelling in a car (see page 67)

LOOKING AFTER A SICK OR INJURED DOG

It is most important to keep a sick or injured dog warm and quiet and to apply the same rules as you would to yourself: plenty of tender loving care. Place the dog's bed in a warm, draught-free location; a well-covered hot water bottle can be very comforting. If the dog is not mobile, provide plenty of layers old newspaper and old blankets and rugs as disposable bedding. Small, frequent meals are far more beneficial than quantities of rich food; four small meals of chicken or fish with rice is the recommended diet.

If the dog is suffering from any sort of discharge, including diarrhoea, you should keep it clean by wiping with damp pads of cotton wool/absorbent cotton.

If your veterinarian supplies any medication for your dog, it must be administered according to the instructions and the full course should be completed. If you dog has had surgery or an accident and has stitches, keep them clean and dry. Stop the dog from licking them. Otherwise, it may pull the stitches out, causing further damage and delaying the healing process. Your veterinarian may supply you with an Elizabethan collar. This fits over the dog's head and prevents it from licking its wound. Most dogs do not take kindly to this collar at first, but after a few hours, they become used to it and settle down. If the dog has a bandage that is going to come into contact with the ground, cover it with a plastic bag or a ready-made shoe, the latter being available at most veterinarians and pet stores.

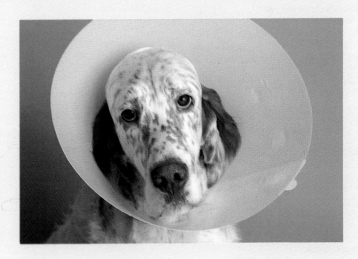

An Elizabethan collar fits around the dog's neck and prevents it licking wounds and pulling at stitches.

INDEX

Page numbers in *italics* refer to captions to illustrations

ACKNOWLEDGEMENTS

The authors would like to thank their editor, Linda Doeser, designer Pedro Prá-Lopez, veterinary consultant John Oliver BVetMed, MRCVS and illustrator Samantha Elmhurst. The photographer would like to thank the processors Colour Centre (London) for processing film with their usual care and efficiency and Aquapets, Ealing for supplying the accessories for photography.